Christ and the Marginalized

Christ and the Marginalized

Bringing Refuge to the Broken

ELIZABETH HERNANDEZ

WIPF & STOCK · Eugene, Oregon

CHRIST AND THE MARGINALIZED
Bringing Refuge to the Broken

Wipf & Stock
An Imprint of Wipf and Stock Publishers
199 W. 8th Ave., Suite 3
Eugene, OR 97401

www.wipfandstock.com

PAPERBACK ISBN: 978-1-6667-0171-5
HARDCOVER ISBN: 978-1-6667-0172-2
EBOOK ISBN: 978-1-6667-0173-9

06/15/21

I dedicate this book to my precious parents,
Victoriano and Flora Hernandez, from whom flourished the
inspiration for the life of this labor of love.

Contents

Acknowledgments

THIS WORK WAS ONLY possible with the amazing partnership of many committed persons. My gratitude goes out to the leaders of Esperanza Health Center during the administration of Dr. Carolyn Klaus; to Dr. Bryan Hollinger, and the former ED, Mary Beth Swan, and staff; to the unequalled partnership of Hispanic clergy such as the late Dr. Manual Ortiz, the late Reverend Fred Estrada, the late Reverend Raul LeDuc, and my dear friend, the Reverend Luis Centeno, who continues to be a source of strength and much encouragement!

I wish to express a very special appreciation for Bryan Dickey, my prodigy and Refuge's acting director, and to Sharon Mangum for her superlative assistance with the lay counseling training modules. Without their practical help during my difficult health challenges, I could not have completed this work. Thanks as well to Carla Contreras, a kind and generous helper. I also want to thank Dr. Rosilyn Smith, who was always willing to provide the best services to our community, and who provided me with the pure wisdom of heaven during times of great need!

I am very grateful for my former colleague and extraordinary friend, Dr. Trina Wisecup, who reminds me "that there are friends who stick closer than a brother"! And my sincere appreciation goes out to Dr. Diane Langberg for her visionary and selfless pursuit for the healing of the people in the city.

Everyone has an angel, and mine arrived in the form of Ruth Emery (Patsy)! Without her encouragement and steady support, this work would not have come this far.

I cannot miss thanking my doctoral advisor, Dr. John Leonard, who assured me to stay calm as he would get me to the finishing line—and beyond—when the time came to offer the project to the wider public for their encouragement.

Acknowledgments

I am also grateful for Missy Gudz; her love and support for all our efforts to help the people she loves in our community is exceptional.

I offer my sincere gratitude to my gifted editors, Kay ben-Avraham and Joshua Casey, who poured out their efforts without limit for the sake of a hurting humanity.

Finally, I thank the people of North Philadelphia, who trusted us and taught us how to help them solve their great challenges.

Introduction

PSYCHOLOGISTS BELIEVE THAT IN human life, the first five years are the "sensitive" ones. Like a seed sown in fertile ground, each of us need healthy nourishment in order to grow and flourish. These life-producing elements are both seen and unseen: that is, empirical and spiritual. While human life is filled with much mystery, I am grateful that it also has evidence-based aspects as well.

My adult life has been spent on the path of the Christ-followers: and specifically, in service to those in the urban context who see themselves as "displaced persons" and whom sociologists label as "marginalized." This identity is not one of victimization—far from it. In my three decades of experience in a counseling ministry in Philadelphia, among the thousands of people I counseled—particularly Hispanics—I witnessed their profound resilience and wholesome community pride. The idea that they were help-less victims went against their worldview—at least, for those from genera-tions born and raised in Puerto Rico and other Latin American countries. Yes, they would concede to the reality of suffering, affliction, family prob-lems, lack of resources, unfamiliarity with American institutions, and the challenges presented by the language and cultural barriers between them and mainstream American culture. But these communities possessed a strength I have not seen equalled before or since.

That strength, I believe, is testament to the movement of Christ among the marginalized. I have seen Christ at work in the lives of those I have counseled; but in truth I encountered him far earlier and more per-sonally than in my adult life and ministry. My girlhood days were spent in the South Bronx, a sociologically deprived community in New York City made famous by *Fort Apache, the Bronx* a film released in 1981 and starring Paul Newman. This movie portrayed a very realistic portrait of the community's plight. Yet despite the realities of suffering, my earliest memories are filled with wonderful, compassionate neighbors, married couples, playmates, Broadway shows, and above all, the dedication and tenderness of my teachers at P. S. 20. In that setting of joy and human warmth in the face of great trials, the seeds of dignity and integrity for humanity were first planted in my soul. And this theme of joy amid suffering, I would come to learn, is the very hallmark of Christ's presence in the lives and world of marginalized peoples.

Just as I learned the power of Christ early in life, so too I learned of the impacts of marginalization. One community that left a profound effect on me is known as Castle Hill, on the east side of the Bronx, where we moved when I was eleven. In the 1970s, this community was primarily middle class: integrated, but mostly Jewish. Across from our new home was a Jewish synagogue, and a few blocks away was the Castle Hill Beach Club. My family was too poor to afford membership for all nine children in our home; and even if that had not been the case, our well-to-do suburban neighbors saw us as the "Other." The pain and stigma of being viewed as Other by a majority culture cut us deeply, as it has always done in years since.

Still, despite hurtful experiences of exclusion, during my teenage years and into my young adulthood, I continued to taste of those same cultural riches I had been welcomed into during childhood. And added to those, I was receiving the faith-based influences of local priests, nuns, and evangelical Christians, increasing and deepening the immense richness of Christ in my life, in the form of repentance, forgiveness, and grace. Adolescence marked for me a passage of much growth in social responsibility, in contributing to family needs, and in learning how to live by the golden rule of "loving thy neighbor as thyself." All things were reconciled in my life during these years. I did not know it at the time, but I was being prepared for a ministry of reconciliation in the next phase of my life.

Entering that phase meant that my understanding broadened, and my awareness of my community's history, challenges, and strengths began to take clearer form as I matured. American majority culture, in response to the Puerto Rican diaspora in the 1950s, formed one image of people from marginalized communities—stereotypes of laziness, entitlement, poor character, and so forth. The more I grew, and the more I saw, the more I recognized what challenges these stereotypes are.

Poverty is a reality for the urban dweller; yet for those born and raised in various Latin American countries, and who migrated to the United States (as in the case of Puerto Ricans) or who immigrated (as is the case for all other Hispanics from Latin republics), to be poor is not "sinful" or "shameful." It is simply a reality of life, and of our human condition—and one that the marginalized are often more aware of than those who belong to majority culture in America. As I encountered these beleaguered believers, I learned to see through the lies of stereotypes to the truth of their identity and character.

The people are *humble*. While the challenges they face are real, an inner foundation holds their lives afloat. Most of them set foot on American shores with little in their hands. What they did have in their "brown bags" was their faith, family, and good work ethic, as well as a strong sense of themselves—of their language, culture, and heritage—and a clear vision of their dreams and hopes. They saw this land as most other immigrants do: as a land of opportunity, improvements, and achievement. The large majority are legal American citizens, as in the case of Puerto Ricans; and others, like those from the Dominican Republic, are proud of their active progress toward becoming American citizens. They share a confidence and aspirations, a freedom to navigate life in their new communities for the betterment of themselves and their families.

There is a Spanish idiom that perfectly captures the hope and vibrant resilience of the people, despite their suffering and adjustments: "*Nunca es tarde, si la dicha es buena.*" In other words, "It is never late, if the outcome is delightful." This idiom implies patience, endurance, long-suffering, disappointments, frustration, and hope. In a nutshell, it is all that the gospel of Jesus Christ promises us: a steadfastness, a waiting, a persevering through trials with courage and strength.

The people are also *courageous*. They travelled to an unknown land, leaving everything that was familiar—their homes, farms, and *colmados*, their churches and relatives, and their cultural symbols and emotional associations—all to reach a dream: the American dream of freedom and opportunity. They actively looked for ways to contribute to and strengthen their new land.

As I learned of this community's strengths, so too I learned of its challenges. The city officials and social agencies where I lived and ministered concluded that there was a "needs gap"; a large number of law-abiding, tax-paying citizens were not receiving proper medical, psychological, or social services because of cultural and language barriers. Urban dynamics and a changing social landscape posed a real threat to these Hispanic families, most of whom came from rural backgrounds. Generalized anxiety and depression disorders began to develop in many of these families; yet still, their sense of self and deep connections to a mature, positive cultural identity remained. To this day, they have no need to apologize for being the "other" or "inferior." They know exactly what they are doing and why they are here.

In a great number of these vibrant marginalized communities, their strong Christian faith shielded many from losing all. People sought new resources and answers to combat the challenges of life in the city: crime, drug and alcohol abuse, substandard housing, low wages or unemployment. They showed themselves to be a courageous people, with a strong work ethic and moral standards which helped them, in the earlier years, to adjust and adapt as best as possible with a humility that still brings tears to my eyes.

In my own entrance into Christian ministry among the marginalized, I soon learned that the greatest assets these communities possess are their religious leaders. Here at the foot of the cross is where all roads meet, breaking down barriers of race, culture, socio-economic status, age, and gender. And our communities did not simply pay lip service to inclusion: all helpers and all help was accepted under the guidance of our top leaders.

In my experience, such inclusion is a great strength on the ground; we certainly needed every single effort. Our leaders—Reverend Doctor Manuel Ortiz (senior pastor, founder of Ayuda Community Center and "Joy in the City," a faith-based school); Reverend Fred Estrada (founding member and executive director of Esperanza Health Center, leader in Hispanic Clergy); and Raul LeDuc (statesman and senior pastor of Iglesias Sion)—all now gone to glory, were truly godly men. They were each first-generation Puerto Ricans in the larger community, and they saw the humanity in everyone they served, believing in our shared nature as made in the image of God, no matter our heritage or backgrounds. All three poured themselves into their congregations and communities for over three decades; all three invested time and finances for the achievement of a master's level seminary education; all three were the founders of other social institutions and statesmen for our people. All three, too, were husbands and fathers.

One member of this prestigious clergy group continues to serve in our community: Reverend Luis Centeno, the recipient of the Robert Wood Johnson community health leadership award (2001) and a member of the Philadelphia Police Chaplaincy Program, serving under former commissioners Charles Ramsey and Richard Ross. Currently, Pastor Centeno is also the Northwest regional director of the National Suicide Foundation. He is the senior pastor of Barnabas Ministry and chaplain for Philadelphia Law

Enforcement. Late in life, he has returned to the classroom and obtained a bachelor's degree in Islamic studies. He is the father of seven children and husband to Elsie.

I mention all this because for the past three decades, my partnership with all of these Hispanic clergy is the greatest testimony of what it is to see Christ at work among the marginalized. In some of these faith-based social outreach ministries in our communities, Christians from all walks of life, socio-economic backgrounds, and age groups—including Christians from wealthier suburban communities—supported our ministries to the urban poor financially, with intellectual capital, with their social networking skills, and by way of direct membership as members of boards. Dr. Carolyn Klaus, founder of Esperanza Health Center, and Dr. Diane Langberg, leading psychologist and cofounder of the Place of Refuge, along with their cohorts, are examples of this collaboration in its preliminary phase. We also partnered with secular organizations such as Concilio for Latinos, HACE, Asociación de Puertorriqueños en Marcha (APM), and Temple University Social Services Research, to name a few: making collective efforts to ameliorate suffering and push back the forces of malevolence.

In my time as a shepherd-helper, working with Christ among the marginalized, I have often felt as though I were walking a dim path, holding a lantern up in the gloom, "leading" in one sense, but more truly simply *accompanying*. Often for those of us in positions of ministry, we can fall into the error of seeing those we are helping through the lens of an "us and them" divide—when in truth, living in this fallen and broken world means that there is no *us* and no *them*. The leaders and the lost alike make up one great *we*—a family, with one head that is Christ. When I have offered guidance to those seeking help, I am usually only one or two steps ahead on the very same path we all walk. This truth is so important to remember, whenever we seek to join the work of Christ among the downtrodden and suffering.

Early on in my ministry, I started to reflect on this truth, together with what I was listening to on a daily basis in my role as a counselor. The hardships of the people I counseled were palpable. Although I was only in my early thirties at the time, I had lived long enough to realize that suffering and hardship would come to every human being, including me. I imagined that perhaps one day, my life or that of my loved ones could encounter health crisis, financial difficulties, betrayal, apathy, or schisms in ministry. Unlike what most are rightfully reasonable to ask—*why me*—my question was, "Why *not* me?" I anticipated suffering and hardship as those I counseled taught me to do. And they also gave me the greatest lesson: we are more than victorious through Christ, who comforts and sustains us. Yet it was not enough for me to simply grasp these truths intellectually or professionally. Soon, I would be tested—personally.

In 2005, the first of two greatest life trials was sent to me. I was diagnosed with multiple sclerosis, and the treatment was severe. Yet my mind was protected from fear, anxiety, depression, or confusion. By now, all the positive accumulative influences in my family of origin, my childhood, and the faith of my adulthood years served to solidify the central hypothesis of my life: belief in Jesus Christ as my Redeemer, my rock, my Life.

Even so, this diagnosis was a surprise, coming as it did at a moment when I was the chosen leader to start a new ministry (the Place of Refuge), and when I was in my second year of my doctoral studies at Westminster Theological Seminary. The pressure was as intense as when I first learned Greek and Hebrew—quite a challenge for a member of a blue-collar interracial community, with only a New York City public school education. I knew this diagnosis meant I would again face a hard and unknown difficulty; but just as I had learned exegesis and translation, so I would have to do the same here. Yet I would not be alone. The people we served for nearly three decades in Philadelphia were my teachers. They had modeled for me the virtues of humility and courage; their dreams to improve their lives for themselves and their children, and their profound desire to work and practice their religion with freedom, decency, integrity, and human dignity, became my compass. And I had learned my lessons well; I knew by now that Christ's way with us is not to spare us from all suffering but to strengthen us to face it.

The second great life trial appeared on April 19, 2020. A month earlier, our country was shut down due to the Covid-19 pandemic. My parents began to feel sick in their home, in the east side of the Bronx. As a former health care executive administrator and counselor, I jumped into a "manager" role. Both my parents tested positive for Covid-19; they were admitted to the hospital and placed in the same room. After my multiple compulsive phone conferences with ER doctors, infectious disease specialists, radiologists, and nurses, and the devastation of the ICU, respirators, plasma therapy, and antibiotics, our father succumbed to the virus, while our mother was miraculously discharged.

Our father, whom we loved with the profoundest reverence, had the absolute best medical care at the attending hospital (Phelps), as did our precious mother. We as their children could not be present to love and care for them from April 19 to May 6; our only consolation was our virtual visits with them on Zoom. We could not say goodbye in person, nor hold a traditional funeral as our ancestors have done since 1493 in Puerto Rico. We had no choice but cremation: a ritual never practiced in our family. The memorial service was conducted on Zoom. Our father had dictated in 2016 his choice of biblical passage, his preferred hymns, and his personal message to his wife, children, and friends.

As the Spanish idiom I quoted earlier says, "It is never late, if the outcome is delightful." In this, too, I have seen the sustaining power of Christ amid suffering. This second great trial happened within the context of the most professional health providers at Phelps Hospital. The excellence of their medical diagnosis and treatments was exceptional. From top to bottom, the personnel—including their CEO and medical specialists—all communicated directly with me with respect and integrity. Seven months have now gone by since the passing of my dear father. To our great joy, our mother survived Covid-19 and is progressively recovering. She is under the tender loving care of my sisters in her new home in Florida.

In his masterpiece, *Exclusion and Embrace*, Miroslav Volf describes the notion of "a double vision." This is when we are able to have one foot deeply rooted inside our own cultures and worldview, with the other foot outside to embrace the "other." As I have come to see through my professional and personal experiences, we learn this double vision most profoundly when we follow in the footsteps of Christ as he moves among the marginalized. Christ, our great Counselor, not only sees the first five years as the most sensitive but in fact sees our entire lives as needing his tender watch. The marriage of the empirical and the spiritual in lay counseling understands the importance of the psycho-social realities that affect those we serve; and at the same time, it also understands deeper truths like those described in 2 Corinthians 4:18 (KJV), which reminds us, "We look not at the things which are seen, but at the things which are not seen; for the things which are seen are temporal; but the things which are not seen are eternal."

Our faith in this promise becomes our lighthouse in the midst of many storms. This learning equips us to live in the world as "wounded healers," even as Christ himself. In the face of the great suffering this world contains, *compassion* is the only word that speaks volumes to a hurting humanity.

It is my hope that the content of this book—along with its practical modules, which focus on simple but important techniques to enable laypeople to extend a helping hand—will bring healing and hope to the hurting and broken among us.

—Elizabeth Hernandez
Philadelphia, PA
November 2020

1

Why Trauma? Why the City?

A HARD-WORKING, MIDDLE-AGED LATINO man, father to six children, recently suffered three heart attacks. His family background is broken, like most of the clients I see. He loves Jesus, but the weight of unemployment and disability has become too much for him. He is bowed down with past pain and present despair.

Look around you. There is a famine in Christian circles for true comfort among the broken and hurting in the body of Christ. All of humanity has been affected by the fall, but those who have undergone trauma feel keenly alone, abandoned by God, and unseen by the people of God. Yet God longs to pour out grace upon those who stand in broken relationship, and they desperately need God to show up. Among the marginalized, Christ can be seen powerfully at work in the lives and hearts of those our society has neglected.

One way this has taken place, as evidence of the character of our God of love, compassion, and grace, is in the formation of centers like the Place of Refuge, a professional counseling center located in the heart of impoverished North Philadelphia, trauma-informed and faith-based. For many years, I served as executive director at this counseling center, and in my time there, I saw the movement of Christ among the marginalized in ways that I will never forget. Our efforts, and the work of Christ, were by no means restricted to this one ministry—in fact, much of what I learned of Christ's ways formed over the course of a pilgrimage: a journey in ministry filled with many waystations, stops and starts, and seasons of new wisdom gathered as I lived and worked within several different ministries. Though

I will write of many of these, I yet offer in these pages an especially close look within the walls of the Place of Refuge as a living, vibrant example—a single image among many—of the healing of Christ poured into the hearts of alienated people.

My client and I prayed together, and I made some calls on his behalf. At the end of our session, his whole countenance had lit up. "You have no idea what this means for me," he said. "If I'm lame when I come, I leap when I leave. If I'm hungry, I leave full. You have God and walk with God, and I know God is here—and that God takes care of me."

In this way, we as the church can help: building a bridge between the sufferer and God, between the hurting community and the church, between the individual and the counselor. That bridge brings an end to famine in people's lives. It means that the sufferer need no longer walk alone.

The journey for many poor communities in our urban areas is sometimes excruciating. At times, the burden may feel so overwhelming that men and women may even despair of life. When a man like this client of mine loses his ability to sustain himself and those who depend on him, and he has no control over his circumstances, the burden accumulates—it becomes heavy—and it can lead to destruction. This is not the story of suffering felt in one dark night of the soul. This is the story of helplessness, of the slow crush of the spirit. It is to have all the *will* to survive and thrive and succeed, but to have no *means* to do so.

The ministry of Christ to these marginalized people is to come alongside, to speak comfort: "We are here with you. We will not leave you until God blesses you." That clasp of a hand in the darkest place is redemptive; and when we offer it, we follow the risen Lord into unique and redemptive work. After all, Christ sees the whole of creation—the broken along with the beautiful—as sacred. Those who follow Christ have a calling from above, and the gifts God gives each of us inform, direct, or confirm that calling. When we step out as the body of Christ, together into the valley of tears, we lift up the Lord Jesus Christ for all people to see.

I tell this story of the Refuge model as one of the many embodiments of Christ—his hands and feet—among those who are downtrodden, as a way to bridge the gap between the mental health profession and people who desire to help the hurting. They know the community: they speak the language, and they understand the culture. By providing these helpers with knowledge of trauma care, soon the broken and abandoned people of their community can receive counseling support from lay people, fellow believers who know how to administer basic counseling skills in a helping relationship.

I will share many things in these pages. First, I will give the scriptural and theological imperative for the kind of counseling work I describe. I will offer a Puerto Rican case study and illuminate its themes through the work of other experts in the field, as well as through the Refuge model, showing how Christ is glorified when secular psychology and faith-based approaches work together in harmony for the benefit of those who are suffering. Furthermore, I will share my own story and the story of the Place of Refuge, introducing readers along the way to basic lay counseling skills, with special emphasis on the true nature of trauma and the reverence in care that it demands, teaching them how to walk alongside those who have been afflicted by unspeakable acts of sin. I will present a vision of the application of both training and the gospel intersecting for the person's healing, as we have experienced it in the development of the Place of Refuge and the training work we have done to date. I will offer in full the Refuge training modules for establishing a lay counseling ministry within a congregation or an organization, which readers can then adapt to fit the needs of their own communities. And finally, I will give voice to the great need in the world today—a need that the church cannot, and must not, ignore.

My own calling is to the broken in my community, the Hispanic population in North Philadelphia. But my work, and the work of the Place of Refuge, can serve as a model for urban ministry through counseling in many contexts—and my hope and prayer is that this book will not only be a resource for the church in North Philadelphia, but also for the church beyond my local community, in other cities where brokenness seems victorious and the need too great.

And here in North Philadelphia, our lay counseling training calls and equips men and women, gifted by our Maker, to go out and feed God's sheep who are hurting and in pain—to work not only with those suffering from trauma, but also to help individuals who ask for guidance and support in daily hardships. As a non-profit, trauma-informed and faith-based center, Refuge provides a quality of professional, clinical care in its counseling services—one living example of Christ at work among the alienated and the marginalized. In accordance with its mission to provide faith-based care for trauma victims, the lay counseling program we developed grew out of a desire to in turn train professional and lay counselors (and communities) in the skills necessary for work with victims of trauma.

God began this work by calling us in a moment of crisis at a local church. These preliminary steps showed us the need to do more. As a first step toward filling that need, we created a training program on how to respond to trauma in a church setting. Over the course of a decade following, we had the opportunity to refine our approach as we presented to various churches and community organizations. Soon another church called upon us in spring 2012 to formalize this training. They sought to strengthen their parishioners through comprehensive lay counseling training and spiritual guidance. In that moment, our goal evolved from a short-term, supplemental effort to become the starting point of a formal lay counseling outreach within a given church. Our meeting became the beginning of a strong relationship between this church and the Place of Refuge in fulfilling the Great Commission. In this way, those who have set their hands to the plow beside Christ's join in common cause together.

We worked extensively with local leaders—especially church leaders—to empower them to assess, help, and at times refer the sufferers who come under their authority. As we did so, we remained rooted in our original undertaking, seeking above all to go into the place of deepest suffering and help bring God's healing there in lasting ways in the lives of the downtrodden. The Refuge staff sought to embody those gifts that make for a great counselor: good listeners, patient, formally educated at secular institutions and seminaries, discerning, measured, and critical. We designed our beautiful office to promote real peace the moment people walk through the door. We used laughter, creating an amiable culture. We kept the space clean and uncluttered, serene and unpretentious. And yet, with all these things in place, even with the strongest curriculum especially tailored for work in this community, we would not have succeeded—not without Jesus Christ our Lord to guide us.

Lay counseling training creates a framework for the most basic and practical steps that can be taken to help a person in need. When leaders within a community have such training, they foster a strong community, a strong fellowship, between the church and her people, between leadership and the voiceless, and between the believer and the seeker.

In the eight modules described in this book, the core curriculum for lay counseling training, we have teaching that is simple, Christian, practical, and relevant to the needs we have encountered in our time serving in the city. The principles, knowledge, and skills involved are in reach for the professionally trained clinician and for the untrained lay person alike. In following these practical, concrete methods of trauma-informed healing efforts, anyone, regardless of background, can learn to recognize and participate in the work of Christ among those who have been alienated.

The modules do not by any means constitute an exhaustive course in counseling. Rather, they serve as a starting point, preliminary work for equipping those who care for the hurting. The Refuge model is a way of helping people carry burdens, a way of walking alongside someone—not of fixing people, and especially not of making ourselves indispensable to their healing. Amy Carmichael, a missionary who spent her life serving and caring for orphans in India, teaches that the desire to reach in and fix people must be fought. She holds up instead the interaction between Jonathan, the son of King Saul, and his friend David who later became king: "And Jonathan Saul's son arose, and went to David into the wood, and strengthened his hand in God" (1 Sam 23:16 KJV). Rather than ministering to David so that Jonathan "becomes necessary to him, [he instead] leaves his friend strong in God, resting in God, safe in God."[1]

Likewise, any lay counseling outreach must leave people with a greater dependency and thirst for God, rather than dependence on the human instrument. This is what we strive to teach, just as we ourselves have learned at the feet of Christ, in his work with the poor.

A Practical Theology: Helping the Urban Poor

The body of Christ has both the privilege and responsibility to care for the least among us, and we cannot turn a deaf ear to the cries of the urban poor, whose socio-economic reality often intensifies the effects of trauma in their lives. No darker stain can be left on a person's body, mind, and spirit as that left by the evil of trauma, which often goes hand-in-hand with poverty. The community we served—primarily Hispanics—did not have a counseling service that could provide culturally appropriate, spiritually sensitive, bilingual, and trauma-informed counseling. What this community *did* have was a committed group of pastors and lay leaders who cared for the suffering of the people. The fields ripe for harvest would have a fresh influx of workers, if only we could first work with these pastors and lay leaders.

Poverty opens the way to the illegal drug trafficking that wreaks havoc in our community. The lure of easy money produces drug addiction and crime. Homicide is rampant. Families crumble. Suffering spreads. In this

1. Carmichael, *Edges*, 5.

manner, trauma takes over a whole community. The need could not be greater, in North Philadelphia and elsewhere, and often, as in our community, caring pastors and lay leaders lack only the knowledge of trauma counseling to equip them to answer that need.

Voices of the Experts

Secular and non-secular experts in the field, in many ways, stand shoulder to shoulder on the profound significance of this issue. Dr. Langberg, a renowned Christian psychologist and speaker, believes that trauma is the mission field of the twenty-first century. Dr. Judith Herman, a leading psychiatrist and author of the celebrated book *Trauma and Recovery*, writes:

> The traumatic event challenges an ordinary person to become a theologian, a philosopher and a jurist. The survivor is called upon to articulate the values and beliefs that she once held and that the trauma destroyed. She stands mute before the emptiness of evil, feeling the insufficiency of any known system of explanation. Survivors of atrocity of every age and every culture come to a point in their testimony where all questions are reduced to one, spoken more in bewilderment than in outrage; *Why?* The answer is beyond human understanding . . . why me?[2]

Dr. Bruce Perry, a neuroscientist in the field of trauma, has researched the effects of trauma on the human brain. He believes that trauma affects children's brains, stating, "Ultimately, what determines how children survive trauma, physically, emotionally, or psychologically, is whether the people around them—particularly the adults—stand by them with love, support, and encouragement."[3] Clearly, this is a simple but courageous call for the average person to take time to care for the most vulnerable in their community.

Dr. Sandra Bloom, another leading expert in the field of trauma treatment, created the Sanctuary model of treatment (first introduced at Friends Hospital in Philadelphia). She writes that "[o]ur ability to form attachments to each other and form social groups has been our best defense and has guaranteed our survival. Attachment to our social group is a deeply ingrained structure that derives from our primate heritage."[4] Trauma renders us helpless and powerless, particularly during childhood

2. Herman, *Trauma and Recovery*, 178.

3. Perry and Szalavitz, *The Boy*, 5.

4. Bloom, *Creating Sanctuary*, 16.

years. It directly affects that ability to attach to our social groups and therefore threatens our survival.

Recognition of this need caused North Philadelphia's leading mental health organization to come to the Place of Refuge and ask us to fill the gap between mental health professionals and those receiving counseling support. They initially expressed interest in the Refuge model's success in the professional counseling sphere, but later, they (and we) realized that this model could also utilize lay people of faith, training and equipping them to administer basic counseling skills in a helping relationship.

The voices of these leading experts form a single conclusion: trauma creates a great need we must meet. It shakes its victims to the core; so, for healing to occur, we must take initiative on behalf of those who have been wounded. It cannot solely be done in individual therapy, though that is crucial. The Refuge model utilizes multiple avenues in its pursuit of healing and care, not replacing but adding onto and strengthening the individual therapeutic model.

Personal Journey: Constructing a Calling

By nature, we search for meaning and seek purpose for our lives. Scripture teaches that we are all made in the image of God, and as such we have been given a mission in life that is uniquely ours. I am no exception: discovering my life's devotion has been a journey, and it is inextricably bound up with the mission of the Place of Refuge and the way we are all transformed when we walk beside Christ as he works with the marginalized.

My parents, young and living simply in a picturesque Puerto Rican country town named Florida, had three children before me. They felt a deep connection to the land, the culture, the language, and the Catholic Church, with its rich traditions. Lured by the hopes of wealth and prosperity waiting in America, however, my parents became part of the mass exodus of Puerto Ricans in the late 1950s, seeking work in New York City's booming manufacturing industry. The spirit of excitement and optimism was strong. As a young child, I heard family members tell each other that New York was so prosperous you could kick dollar bills down the street with your boots.

The fantasy gave way to reality as my parents went through the assimilation process in Brooklyn. They struggled to adjust to the cold weather. (Sadly, my mother learned about this the hard way as she stepped outside our tenement building in zero-degree weather without a winter coat. For the rest of her life, she had chronic asthma, which threatened her life during my birth.) We lived in an enclave of newly arrived workers like ourselves, people clustered in groups mirroring the neighborhoods they had formed back in Puerto Rico. They lived by a deeply entrenched worldview: faith, family, work ethic, and responsibility to the larger community.

Our family later moved to the east side of the Bronx in an integrated community known as Castle Hill. The Roman Catholic Church had a prominent position in our community and our home. My mother was a homemaker and my father worked in a New Jersey factory—a two-hour commute every day. In many ways, my parents gave us a beautiful home life. With both parents always by our side, we enjoyed the strong points of our culture, such as music, language, food, and the good company of family and friends. My parents struggled financially, with (by then) nine children, but we managed to survive and held our heads up high—until my older brother José got caught up with the wrong crowd.

My father was burdened with his own anxieties, as he took his role as provider very seriously. He and my brother had a combative relationship, which broke the peace of our home. José also began to fight with Nydia, my eldest sister, who took seriously the cultural role of responsibility toward her younger siblings. Our home, still joyful at times, grew highly stressful.

Then, in 1977, our family went through one of the most horrific forms of suffering any family can ever experience: the death of a child. Through this death, the gospel of Jesus Christ reached my heart, and later the hearts and minds of most of my immediate family. My little sister Janet was born with a serious heart condition. She had three major open-heart surgeries. At seven years old, she made medical history as the first young recipient of a plastic valve. Major magazines such as *Life* and *Time* wrote about this trailblazing medical accomplishment. Perhaps this was part of her mission in life, to open a way for others to receive modern and improved medical treatment. Despite these measures, however, she did not survive her third surgery.

Our world turned upside down with her death. In a train station one day, bereaved and grieving, I met a young man who would have a permanent impact in my life forever. A devout Christian and eager to share his faith with me, he introduced me to his parents and grandmother, who displayed the gospel of Jesus Christ in both word and deed. I still remember the day I walked into their home. It felt like nothing I had ever experienced in my life or within my own culture. Although the Rodriguez family spoke Spanish, looked like us, and kept a Puerto Rican home in a way I recognized, the atmosphere of their home seemed different. What peace was present there! It had the air of a monastery, with Christian books, a piano, hymnals, and daily meals shared by the family and their guests.

In that home, I first saw the sanctification of my culture. The *shalom* of God gripped my heart. The Rodriguez family was not perfect; oddly, seeing their imperfections convinced me that this *shalom* was beyond them: that it came *through* their family but not *from* them. They prayed, read the Word of God, and made their home a sanctuary of worship, a place where people in need were welcomed and loved. They took me in to live with them during my last year of college, and with their help, I learned the secret of this *shalom*: they introduced me to Christ.

Tragedy had not finished with our family, however. My brother José continued with the wrong crowd, experimenting with heroin and ultimately ending his life at age twenty-seven. He had reconciled with my father the year before, and we had known renewed peace in relationship with him. But when he passed, my parents—new believers at the time—were at a loss to understand this awful death. We all grieved bitterly that someone so young and bright should be gone.

In this way, through immersion in the culture and exposure to its poverty and crime, and through the experience of personal tragedy, by the time I entered the workforce as a counselor, I had a painful firsthand knowledge of the social struggles this population faces on a daily basis. Yet I also had the powerful *shalom* of God and the direct knowledge that Christ can transform a life. I wanted deeply to bring these riches to my culture in its brokenness.

I studied at Baruch College for my undergraduate degree in psychology and Puerto Rican studies. In 1989 I left my job, subletting my apartment in the East Bronx. My first mentor, the late Mrs. Barbara Archilla, my pastor's wife, was my greatest supporter. She attended Westminster Theological Seminary in their doctorate of ministry program, and she knew that God was leading me into counseling with the Hispanic community. Any counseling education I undertook, she told me, should be in a school that was faithful to Scripture. And so I enrolled at Westminster for a master's degree in religion, majoring in counseling. Incredible fruit came from this time: I learned two classical languages (Greek and Hebrew) in addition to my Spanish and English. Slowly, I developed a Christian worldview. I learned to incorporate biblical principles into counseling.

My calling formed gradually, nurtured by mentors and study, and characterized by singleness. In our contemporary times, singleness is under-appreciated and marriage and family overrated. Scripture, on the contrary, upholds both marriage and singleness as having great value, and I have known the great value in my own life of purity in single living. Because of my choice to remain single, Christ took preeminence in me—an experience many throughout the church's history have spoken to. Although I have dated, developed many friendships, and remained close with family and friends in New York, I have above all wanted Jesus Christ, and for me, this has meant a life called to singlehood. I discovered my calling from that place of love—and I found it, in practical terms, in the people of North Philadelphia.

Ministerial Journey: Developing Refuge

The vision for the Place of Refuge began nearly seventeen years ago, while I was working as a bilingual counselor at Esperanza Health Center. As a public health agency, Esperanza struggled to meet the needs of the Hispanic people in North Philadelphia. Existing counseling models could not encompass the worldview of the majority of our Hispanic clients, many of whom were functionally illiterate and found a strict clinical approach incomprehensible. In some instances, clients actively resisted the methods of counseling employed by mainstream psychotherapists: wanting Spanish-led sessions, less formality, and professional, but warm interaction. Fur-thermore, clients wanted us to understand the role that faith played in their daily lives, and the significance that cultural environment had on their personal experience.

Soon it became clear that the existing models were bankrupt in the face of these needs. The people who came to us did not require another mainstream solution, but instead a faith-based, trauma-informed treatment center that had the flavor of the community it served. After fourteen years of service, I resigned from my position as Director of Counseling at Espe-ranza Health Center to co-found the Place of Refuge with Dr. Langberg.

The Place of Refuge was first incorporated as a 501(c)3 non-profit counseling center in 1999 as both the need and fruitfulness of this min-istry became apparent. I became its executive director in 2004, and until 2008, we operated out of various borrowed or shared spaces across North Philadelphia. Late in 2007, in collaboration with local government, many area foundations, and donors, we successfully converted a vacant building on the 2900 block of Fifth Street into the vibrant counseling and training center it has become today.

This ministry, many years in the making, arose in answer to a need: a need that could not be answered with mainstream solutions. Refuge formed in the very heart of the Hispanic community, deeply rooted in the lives of local men and women, and in partnership with indigenous leadership—speaking the language, both literally and figuratively, of the sufferer.

Contextualization: Recognizing and Answering the Need

Philadelphia's neighborhoods teem with hurting people, desperate for help. In our community, as elsewhere, marginalized citizens often carry the weight of perceived inferiority from broader culture's systemic exclusion. In our city, 24.5 percent of the population live below the federal poverty line, which is the highest rate among the country's ten largest cities.[5] Poverty and mental health among minority populations appear to be often linked, as one study found: 49 percent of black and 61 percent of Hispanic clients live in high-poverty areas, as opposed to 15 percent of whites.[6] These individuals suffer from broken families, crime and violence, unemployment, and the prevalence of drug abuse, with its effects both social and personal. In 2015, our neighborhood and others like it in North Philadelphia had unemployment rates between 21–40 percent,[7] compared to 5.2 percent citywide.[8]

The statistics do not sufficiently capture the despair that still haunts life in the inner city. The urban poor lead desperate lives, fighting for their very survival. Their battle with education, especially, is profound: Pennsylvania's graduation rate for Hispanic students in 2015 was only 69 percent, while the national rate for Hispanic students was 78 percent. The state's graduation rate for African American students was 71.8 percent, while its overall graduation rate was 84.8 percent. White graduation rates in the state, meanwhile, were at 89.3 percent.[9]

In many cases, young people simply do not have the tools to deal with parenting, addictions, abuse, mental health problems, violence, and other trauma. The problems only increase as they grow older. Social services

5. "Philadelphia 2020," 2.
6. Chun-Chung Chow et al., "Racial/Ethnic Disparities."
7. "Philadelphia's Labor Force."
8. "Philadelphia 2020," 5.
9. "2017 Building a Grad Nation," 19–20, 47, 49.

available to the poor often fall short in quality and relevance to the demographic; yet these are the people who need help the most. The Place of Refuge is designed to give them help and hope, one broken heart at a time.

How do ministries like the Place of Refuge accomplish this—and, more importantly, how can the process be duplicated, both in this community and in others like it? Any theological framework applied to a particular community means treading carefully through a narrowly defined practical theology. Wisdom cries for harmonious interaction between God and humanity, evidenced in how God speaks to a people group through the lens of their identity and place in the world. The apostle Paul, for example, utilized such wisdom when he spoke to the people of Athens in Acts 17, using their altar "to an unknown god" as a starting point for preaching the gospel. In order for a Christian to minister effectively to the brokenness, suffering, pain, and affliction of an individual, the proper contextualization of Scripture is needed. Even armed with the best intentions, a theology that lacks a comprehensive biopsychosocial[10] contextualization can cause more harm than good. After all, how else can we minister to people if not through their own reality?

Any goal of ministry, in such a context, must first begin with a solid understanding of the target group. To fully illustrate our starting point for relevant biblical counseling, then, we will here explore concepts of marginalization for the people we serve in North Philadelphia, and we will also examine the role that trauma plays in their daily lives.

Setting the Stage: The Puerto Rican Context

In order for us to understand the experience of the marginalized—the outsiders—I would like to briefly point to the historical religious experience of other ethnic groups in American society. In R. Laurence Moore's book *Religious Outsiders and the Making of Americans*, he focuses on the historical patterns of ethnicity and contemplates religious differences. His reflection was rooted in what dictates historical relevance in the areas of

---

10. A *biopsychosocial* is a comprehensive assessment used at the beginning of treatment in a mental health setting. It provides a thorough history of the individual's profile—including social environment, religious beliefs, family of origin, and basic mental health status—and it provides a framework for the development of a treatment plan, which is written collaboratively by the counselor and the individual seeking help.

ethnicity and spirituality.[11] Moore starts from Will Herberg's conclusion that "American religious life has been headed for a broad and tolerant religious accommodation characterized, first, by a homogenizing of ethnic traits that has made all Protestants alike, all Catholics alike, and all Jews alike; and second, by the development of a common faith that has bonded these three large groups together."[12]

Moore comes to the conclusion that the key to understanding religious experience in the United States is a sense of harmony and unity among denominations, which eclipses individuality. That is to say, consensus overrules pluralism, consensus being the glue that holds the whole tapestry of religious life in America together. The practice of religious belief creates a tie of religious experience, one that does not include those outside the theological boundaries of that faith tradition. In opposition to this, mainstream American society has increasingly sought to enforce the popular idea of "the melting pot": a broader identification with shared American destiny that overrules crippling pluralism.[13]

In those ethnic groups outside of the American mainstream—especially in the time following the American Civil War in the later waves of European migration, e.g., Irish and Italian Roman Catholics, Mormons, European Jews, and so forth—we see in the arrival of these groups a presence that is at times antagonistic to the Protestant mainstream (mostly Episcopalians and Presbyterians). This presence often prompted the ruling or normative groups of that time to redouble their emphasis on their united religious life and to preserve their dominance by economic, political, and legal means, as necessary.[14] Yet insider attempts to check the incoming counter-cultural influences of the presumed outsiders did not always succeed, as outsiders exerted cultural influence, overturning "hierarchies of significance."[15] In response, those original insiders attempted to justify their authority even as their values were unpopular.

However, in time, the grip of the insiders loosens. As worldviews pass from one generation to the next, a more politically welcoming and accepting worldview prevails. The former outsiders, like new wood grafted into a tree, eventually merge with the other branches and become insiders themselves.

11. Moore, *Religious Outsiders*, x.

12. Moore, *Religious Outsiders*, 99.

13. Moore, *Religious Outsiders*, ix.

14. Moore, *Religious Outsiders*, xiii.

15. Moore, *Religious Outsiders*, xiii-xiv.

This ability of those outside the mainstream to assert they are American occurs even as they preserve vestiges of their cultural distinctiveness.[16]

Most cultures that have migrated to the United States have, in this way, assimilated and become American citizens. Why is this not the case with the Puerto Ricans, who have become "stuck" in their identification as a marginalized group? Several reasons contribute to this lack of progression: first, they display a resistance to being assimilated into mainstream American society because of their intense love and loyalty toward their cultural heritage and homeland. Second, their political arrangement under the Puerto Rican commonwealth has in a sense protected this decision as well, making it possible for them to retain two identities at once: Puerto Rican heritage, and American citizenship.[17]

Throughout history, there have been marginalized groups in any given society; present-day America is not an exception to this rule. The dynamics present in the Puerto Rican community of North Philadelphia can serve as a case study in marginalization, with applicability extending far beyond the borders of Philadelphia itself. I will give a brief review here of that history as it pertains to their status as marginalized citizens.

In 1493, when Columbus undertook his second journey to the Americas, he landed in a place we now know as the Caribbean. One of the lush islands he "discovered" is today called Puerto Rico. Two indigenous tribes inhabited the island: the Taino and the Arawak. For the first few centuries after Columbus's arrival, the Spanish empire colonized and ruled over these people. The Spaniards immigrated in large numbers, importing Roman Catholicism, the Spanish language, and other European cultural traditions. A worldview formed, and within this worldview, the indigenous people developed a sense of identity and a sense of their place in the world. Although the African slave trade did not flourish in Puerto Rico as it did in the neighboring islands of the Dominican Republic and Cuba, slavery was established for many years. Over time, German, Irish, and French immigrants

16. Moore, *Religious Outsiders*, xv.

17. Puerto Ricans are known as "rainbow people" because of their high rate of interracial marriages, where families may have members that represent many different ethnicities. The Spanish word *triguenita* refers to a woman of medium-dark skin tone—the complexion held as most desirable—with the figure of *la mujer triguena* celebrated in traditional music, poetry, and oral storytelling. The full embrace of those of African or indigenous descent has been common throughout the generations, such that these cultures have mingled and blossomed within Puerto Rican communities in the form of cuisine, music, literature, religious practice, and social customs.

also arrived in Puerto Rico, intermarrying with the island's residents and leading to an open forum for multiculturalism now deeply entrenched in the Puerto Rican mindset. At the end of the nineteenth century, this would change in radical and unexpected ways.

At the conclusion of the Spanish-American war in 1898, Puerto Rico (as one of the spoils of that war) was handed over to the United States of America. In the twinkling of an eye, the island was plunged into a state of chaos in all aspects of its existence. Seemingly overnight, Puerto Rico transitioned from monarchy to democracy; from Roman Catholicism to Protestantism; from Spanish to English; from European power to American rule; and from communal identity to the American philosophy of individualism. People whose identity had formed under the influence of one context now found themselves living in a diametrically opposed reality.

From 1898 to 1917, the Puerto Rican people did not belong to any particular country, including the United States of America; the Jones Act in 1917 finally granted them American citizenship. During the fifties, there was widespread migration of Puerto Ricans into the continental United States. Most of this migration occurred through a political and economic policy adopted in 1952 known as Operation Bootstrap. The two governments (the Puerto Rican governor, under the newly founded commonwealth status of the *Estado Libre Asociado*, and the United States Congress) agreed that American businesses could go to Puerto Rico and develop businesses there with a tax exemption. During this time, American economic prosperity opened the doors for Puerto Ricans to travel to the United States and get jobs in industry and retail. These migrants were not educated people; they were laborers, farmers, sugarcane workers, and those from the coffee industry. Since they occupied a lower socioeconomic stratum, many of them lived in inner-city neighborhoods throughout the United States, with the highest concentrations in New York, New Jersey, Illinois, and Connecticut.[18]

Although migration from Puerto Rico to the United States mainland continues, current communities now consist primarily of the descendants of those migrant workers. Unlike mainstream American citizens, however, those first Puerto Ricans and their modern descendants were not raised with the reigning cultural influences of America at large (individualism, democracy, the Protestant work ethic, etc.). In other words, although Puerto

18. Baker, *Understanding*, 39. Per Baker on page 47, according to 2000 census data, Florida is now second in numbers of Puerto Ricans to New York (with New Jersey in third place).

Ricans are technically Americans, they are still seen as "other," by themselves and by the rest of society—two different viewpoints that mutually reinforce each other. When migrant families moved to the United States, they may have shared citizenship with other Americans, putting them on the same legal footing as their neighbors, but they did not share much else. They were marked as foreign, and, as often happens in such situations, they banded together in solidarity and cultural resistance to the larger society whenever that larger society alienated them.

What Are the Issues? Marginalization's Effect

As briefly outlined above, the Hispanic community in North Philadelphia faces a multitude of issues: domestic, sexual, and child abuse; drug trafficking; STDs; poverty; mental health issues; gang violence; and addiction, to name a few. These symptoms of marginalization at work in a people group take ugly forms in the lives of individuals.

I see the fall as having done the greatest damage among my patients with inaccurate or distorted identities. For many Hispanics, identities are found in lesser things (medical diagnoses or handicaps, psychological disorders), and the implications lead to a lifestyle of sin as the individual accepts things about herself that could otherwise be changed or improved.

Many of the individuals I counseled had developed identities around their mental and medical diagnoses: major depressive disorder, post-traumatic stress disorder, or—especially common in this community—general anxiety disorder. Often, these diagnoses are the strongest formative influences on people's worldviews and self-conceptions. Whenever a psychological diagnosis acts as a defining factor in the life of a person, chances are that any development of other aspects of the self has been hampered. Patients hold such diagnoses close to the heart with the idea, "This is who I am," and often this can hinder personal growth. While I have deep compassion for those who face mental and/or medical suffering (so much so that I have chosen a ministry of holistic counseling), my hope is that diagnoses will not be the governing factor in forming my patients' identities. I strive to help them see themselves in ways that are more enriching than a professional's diagnosis, ways that could enable them to bear up under their sufferings and seek long-term wholeness.

Another facet of the fall's impact on identity can be seen in the way many individuals limit themselves according to prescribed gender roles.

For Hispanic women in particular, finding identity and human value merely through the rigidity of traditional gender roles limits their personal growth, holding them back from identity transformation. The soil for the nurturance of identity for the Hispanic woman is centered on her relationship with her family. The traditional role society expects her to play during early childhood is one of submission with all male figures: father, brothers, uncles, male cousins, and so forth. She must attend to household duties, such as cleaning and cooking, and if she has any siblings, she is to nurture and care for them. As young women, Latinas are behaviorally trained to flirt, to maximize sexual appeal and still be able to do work at home. A girl's physical appearance rules who she is to herself and to the men in her life (ultimately, her husband).[19] Her role dictates that she appear feminine (make-up, manicured nails, a certain tone of voice and walking style, and sexy clothes). Generally my female patients strive to achieve their culture's unwritten codes for gender roles, regardless of age and body type.

These women continue to have their lives defined by family ties as they grow older. The Puerto Rican core societal value is family: the more children the better, even if childbearing occurs outside of marriage. Infants are adored in this culture, so that even if an unmarried woman has a baby, the child is seen as a blessing.

Whenever I counsel a Puerto Rican woman in the midst of a crisis over an unexpected pregnancy, rarely does she speak of abortion as her first choice. In fact, in some of my former Christian counseling jobs, too many of our young teenage patients were trying to get pregnant, seeking help from our medical staff to plan a pregnancy. Even the mothers of most teenagers look on teenage pregnancy with a certain acceptance.

Puerto Ricans view a single woman's status (especially as she matures) as "perplexing," evidenced by the constant barrage of matchmaking attempts made on her behalf. Romantically attached, she is socially accepted; single, or barren, she poses a problem to society. It is inconceivable that she remains single and without children. There exists no category for a woman on her own, and any who find themselves thus feel the intense pressure.

For this reason, most young women—even in the church—will not obey the standard of holiness set by their faith community, i.e., the call to wait on the Lord for a life partner. The idea that she may have the gift of singleness (even if for a season) does not even cross her mind, and, as social

---

19. Fontes, *Sexual Abuse*, 40–42. In my professional counseling experience with Latina women, I have also empirically observed these patterns.

and family pressures intensify, most of my unmarried female patients ultimately compromise on their *ideal* for a mate in favor of whoever is readily *available*, in essence opening themselves to much suffering.

In short, "femininity," as Hispanic culture defines it, is celebrated, and any departure from it carries social consequences. In the current morality of our times, those with different sexuality are social outcasts in many Hispanic circles—they bring shame to their family. Many families simply remain in denial when a member of the family does not fit the expected mold, and often they avoid the matter altogether until a crisis appears. Such denial and avoidance is complicated by the fact that such issues are now at the center of American culture.

Although Hispanics are less open than most white Americans about discussing sexual topics, my experience in counseling confirms that Hispanic families do often have members who are not traditional in this way, at the same rates as all other groups. I believe that the church can play a key role in ministering to the needs of individuals and families challenged by these realities.

Gender and role identity for males also lies at the center of family life. Generally, Hispanic men are close to their parents, but most males are closer to their mothers. Many enjoy being fathers, but few understand the responsibilities involved in parenting their children. Often the males are discriminated against in broader American society and feel the pressures of marginalization more intensely in this arena. Their work ethic seems weak at times, perhaps because of social and economic realities, but also because of the sense of emasculation that many have experienced in society. Not many are in political or economic positions of power, and they feel their alienation from self deeply. Many suffer from repressed anger and show significant emotional vulnerability where it pertains to interpersonal relationships, while the women have to shoulder the burden of keeping the family together, being strong and long-suffering. Alcohol and drug abuse runs rampant, as does the misuse of sex. These men tend to have very few healthy coping mechanisms, which may explain the high levels of addictions and physical abuse within the Hispanic community.

This last—physical abuse, especially of women and children—is by far the most tragic form of personal alienation I have seen in our service area.[20]

---

20. Comas-Diaz, "Puerto Ricans," 40. Comas-Diaz believes that the *machismo/marianismo* paradigm bears profound implications for sexual abuse.

It represents a problem of epidemic proportions and will be addressed later in this book's discussion on trauma.

As we have seen, gender roles among Puerto Ricans tend to be tightly structured. Sexual structuring for boys and girls begins at the deepest level during childhood. Males are taught to be leaders and females to be submissive,[21] an obvious distinction between the sexes that ultimately forms patterns so pervasive that they carry into adulthood. This line of sex role demarcation creates a double moral standard known as the "*machismo/marianismo* paradigm."[22]

Machismo, as defined by Lillian Comas-Diaz, is "maleness or virility . . . but culturally it means that the man is the provider, and is responsible for the welfare, honor, dignity, and protection of the family."[23] In practical terms, expectations for males include: strength, authority, independence, courage, power, and sexual conquest. The extreme form of *machismo* occurs when the male uses excessive dominance over the woman, abuses alcohol, and is sexually unfaithful or promiscuous.[24] Aggressive, abusive Puerto Rican men reveal a broken masculinity in their cultural identity. They are considered "macho": cool, hip, flirtatious, and smooth. Men who employ *machismo* reap devastating consequences in their spirituality. This form of manliness is at odds with godliness and health at the individual and communal levels.

For centuries, Puerto Rican culture has been influenced by a Roman Catholic worldview, which has created a form of behavior for women: *marianismo*. The closest literal English translation is "Mary-ism." The concept teaches "that women are spiritually superior to men and therefore capable of enduring all suffering inflicted by men."[25] As contrasted to extreme *machismo*, girls are expected to be sentimental, gentle, intuitive, fragile, submissive, and dependent. This image infuses great nobility into daily experiences of sacrifice and suffering for their children, because motherhood is seen as sacred. Abuse in many forms at the husband's hands is seen as

---

21. Comas-Diaz, "Puerto Ricans," 40.

22. Comas-Diaz, "Puerto Ricans," 40–41.

23. Comas-Diaz, "Puerto Ricans," 40.

24. Comas-Diaz, "Puerto Ricans," 40. This component of *machismo*, says Comas-Diaz, can lead to sexual harassment—and even to sexual abuse—under the pretense of gender roles and cultural expectations.

25. Comas-Diaz, "Puerto Ricans," 40. *Marianismo* is based on the Catholic worship of the Mother Mary, virgin and Madonna. It is a code that honors women who abide by it.

spiritual virtue. I have heard even local pastors expressing this belief. As a result, the Puerto Rican woman lives caught in a paradoxical dynamic known as the "Madonna/whore complex": she must be sexually alluring, even aggressive, to please her husband, while at the same time maintaining the inner purity of the virgin.[26] The Madonna/whore often becomes the Madonna/victim in most instances. The only other typical female gender role available to women, however, is *hembrismo* (literally, "femaleness"):

> *Hembrismo* is a natural reaction to *marianismo* and shares common elements with the women's movement in the area of social and political goals . . . [it] connotes strength, perseverance, flexibility, and an ability to survive. However, it can also translate into the Puerto Ricena's attempt to fulfill her multiple role expectations as a mother, wife, worker, daughter, and member of the community.[27]

She is a survivor: strong, flexible, and able to persevere. Yet the life of the *hembrista* is not one of peace—it is one of tension, of defending one's turf, of being tough, being a superwoman. So, for a Puerto Rican woman who is both a housewife and a professional, she plays the *mariana* at home (suffering, victimized, taken for granted) but shifts to a *hembrista* at work. The woman feels acutely the burden of these contrasting cultural demands, and her identity, whether as a doormat or as a hardened survivor, is a far cry from the beautiful identity God has offered to her.

Broken Relationships: Social Alienation and the Fall

The people in our service area celebrate the Puerto Rican Day Parade out in the streets, as mostly teenage boys and girls ride in their cars with thousands of Puerto Rican flags flying. Fifteen years ago, when I lived in a street nearest to the heart of the Puerto Rican enclave, I felt amazed at the nationalistic phenomena. While the parade is held in Center City, the real celebration occurs in the local neighborhoods where friends and families meet to celebrate. Spray-painted automobile rear windows display inscriptions of towns in Puerto Rico where families had their beginnings. Unlike the Fourth of July for dominant American culture, this isolated celebration points to the social alienation that the people experience from mainline culture.

---

26. Comas-Diaz, "Puerto Ricans," 40.
27. Comas-Diaz, "Puerto Ricans," 41.

The marginalization felt by the Puerto Rican community in relationship to the American way of life creates lingering resentment. Their own cultural patterns of Spanish language, Spanish food, Spanish and island music, and the general conviviality of spirit around family and friends stand uninvited into majority American culture. From the viewpoint of a Puerto Rican, rejection from mainstream America serves as a source of great sadness, even turmoil and depression, as evidenced in the lives of many of my patients. Nicholas Wolterstorff writes that "the denial of respect may itself constitute the wound that provokes nationalism . . ."[28] And in North Philadelphia, the Puerto Rican community has suffered from multiple wounds.

In addition to the rejection felt on a national level, many Puerto Ricans also undergo social alienation within their families. Mothers suffer for the welfare of their children and from their husbands' transgressions. They feel lonely. Men feel angry. Both are depressed. This becomes compounded in situations of sexual abuse within a family. Victims often face the worst social alienation, as the family sacrifices the victims' well-being and rights for the sake of keeping the peace. Our senior citizens live alone in despair, without the support of family and friends. The generation gap causes the distancing of parents from their children, and broader social changes, especially in the last two generations, have been detrimental to the Puerto Rican family as a whole.

Puerto Ricans form one of the underclass groups in America.[29] Without access to the opportunities of the majority culture, the people feel abandoned by social and political structures and those in leadership. Many develop depression and anxiety disorders. Most of the counseling I did during my first years in this community involved crisis intervention for those who struggle with suicidal ideation. Many families have been deeply affected by crime and violent bereavement. The poverty level and subsequent economic hardships further add to their alienation.

Broken Relationships: Environmental Alienation and the Fall

The most deeply embedded experience, yet most unidentified for the majority of Puerto Ricans in Philadelphia and elsewhere in the United States, is displacement. As described earlier, most Puerto Ricans currently living in the continental United States came out of need and poverty, leaving their

28. Wolterstorff, *Until Justice*, 105.

29. Massey and Denton, *American Apartheid*, 12.

homeland behind. Today, the commonwealth of Puerto Rico exists at neo-colonization status within the purview and dominion of the United States. Tight control of the economic and political laws in-country allows the United States to keep the Puerto Ricans in a subordinate position of power.

Psychologists now understand the effect of political oppression on a people group, and the American Puerto Rican community in North Philadelphia is a perfect case in point. Those born and raised in Puerto Rico had a self-assurance that began to erode in the next generation, who were born and raised in the mainland United States. Extended exposure to oppression ultimately results in a society internalizing their subordination through loss of will, lack of care for the environment or community, and widespread despair and powerlessness.[30] The people learn that striving does not result in success. All natural, God-given desires for honorable work, supporting one's family, investing in the community, and so forth, only remain in the form of frustrated hopes. And these lead, in time, to patterns like those discussed above—abuse, distrust of authority, unemployment, addictions, mental and physical handicaps. Stripped of neighborhood pride, countless North Philadelphian communities consist of streets littered with trash and graffiti. Crime rates soar, and the local law enforcement's designated label for this area—"The Badlands"—does little to improve the image of the Hispanic community.

My contextual framework for this tension began as a new Christian in the Bronx, at Iglesia Espanola Evangelica. Sermons were steeped in God's Word, preached in beautiful Spanish—complete with cultural metaphors and illustrations, and referencing Latin American poetry. Reverend Archilla was uniquely Latin with a highly informed theology based on the gospel, yet possessing a controlled, deep, tender sentimentalism toward his community. He balanced the intense spirituality of his style with intellect and poetry. Indigenous leadership with integrity marked that New York experience for me, which I have rarely seen duplicated in other communities in which I have lived, including Philadelphia.

The wonder of this church—for others as well as myself—was the dismantling of the secular, oppressive systems of injustice and exclusion, which place mainland Puerto Ricans living in the United States in a marginalized underclass status.[31] From a psychological perspective, the church held us all to a high standard of personal conduct, despite New York's overall negative

---

30. Fontes, *Sexual Abuse*, 34.
31. Massey and Denton, *American Apartheid*, 12.

perception of us as a cultural group. For me, this marked the beginning of a theological foundation for praxis in the church and the Puerto Rican community. Everyone saw the beauty and majesty of Almighty God, and we reached a growing awareness of the fact that we are all made in the image of this awesome and holy God, regardless of how secular American culture systematically diminished us as a people. This migrant community experienced the best of a contextualized form of Christianity: one that spoke to the hearts and minds of Hispanics while bringing forth the strength of their cultural values. These two realities were inextricably related, fostering a sense of self-importance and identity, and connecting the people to the efficacy of the work of God.

A North American worldview—and cross-cultural conflicts—were notably absent from this church experience. The gospel's delivery had a wonderful Caribbean flavor of the Old Spanish world and rhythms. The systemic practices of exclusion, observed in a dominant culture over a subordinate culture, were absent. In keeping with traditional Hispanic worldview and values, sin was not merely an individual affair; it was understood as affecting the whole community. People were free to experience liberty and spiritual growth, which led to psychological and spiritual peace. The church did not operate as a patriarchy; instead, women were leaders and seen as integral to communal life. Members managed to avoid ethnocentrism by their mindfulness of the tensions inherent in being firmly rooted in Hispanic culture and living in a varied American cultural context. Finally, the community did not exist in isolation from the larger context of the body of Christ, nor from the rest of New York society. Possibly because the pastor was a founder of a seminary in San Jose, Costa Rica, an author, and a long-standing translator for Billy Graham in Latin America, the people respected him, and his messages had great relevance for modern life. The *shalom* of God was restored within the walls of the church.

This pastor preached the gospel to us in words and phrases reflecting on our lives. Consequently, spiritual transformation occurred as parishioners learned to apply biblical truth and principles in all aspects of their lives, demonstrating that for them, "religious life *is* life, and not simply an isolated part of life."[32] The preaching of the gospel in their own cultural context directly impacted their work ethic. Many in this congregation were linguistically limited and of humble beginnings, but from one generation to the next, most experienced upward mobility into the mainstream of society

---

32. Nida, *God's Word*, 25.

in New York City through hard work and educational training. Some were lawyers, a few were doctors, and others were educators or business people. A significant number were blue-collar workers who worked in their jobs until retirement. I was also pleasantly surprised to discover that most of the members of this congregation owned property.

While twenty-five years separate my experience in New York City from my experience in Philadelphia, the community dynamics have not changed. My time of ministry in Philadelphia has only increased my understanding of Puerto Ricans in urban America, and my experience with Iglesia Espanola Evangelica showed me how the church can heal great brokenness in a specific cultural context such as this.

Empathy in Light of the Gospel: Christianity's History of Marginalization

Within Christianity, a significant history of alienation is also present, offering a perfect opportunity for empathic connection with those who are marginalized in modern-day societies. There have been many points throughout the centuries when Christians existed only as a fringe group within greater secular society. These marginalized spiritual ancestors of ours were the ones responsible for the beginning of the new American nation—and, far earlier, for the beginning of Christianity itself. Yet today, especially in America, Christians rarely live lives of marginalization. Often, the church strongly aligns itself with its American citizenship, sometimes even more powerfully than it aligns itself with its heavenly citizenship— and in the world today, American citizenship is a position of privilege and power, not marginalization. Yet we must ask ourselves: is this prioritization biblical, or even permissible? Have we lost touch with something, in our lives of comfort and opportunity: something that the marginalized Puerto Rican community is never permitted to forget?

In an April 30, 1944 letter written from his prison cell to his friend, Eberhard Bethge, Dietrich Bonhoeffer admits his struggle in working out "who Christ really is, for us today."[33] The depth of this question comes clearer when seen against the background and context in which Bonhoeffer found himself. Bonhoeffer was a Christian, of course, but also a German. He wrote from a prison cell in Nazi Germany near the height of World War II, less than a year before Berlin's fall to Soviet forces—and his own

33. Bonhoeffer, *Letters*, 279.

execution. Selby shows that Bonhoeffer set forth two rigorous criteria to establish an answer to his question about the person of Christ in today's world: "Christian faith has to address a world in which everyday activity is undertaken on largely secular assumptions; and the gospel has to address human beings in their strength rather than creating and then exploiting a sense of weakness."[34] In other words, Bonhoeffer sought a language of faith connected to reality, a faith to embolden the best of us.

All of this has great relevance to the American church today, and to our responsibility as believers in this world. Pilgrim theology, which I will explore further in chapter 2, has profound significance for all those who seek to join Christ's work among the poor. It resonates with those who seek our help as they wrestle with their Christian character and beliefs and how they interact with the broader society around them, and it has significant, powerful implications to those who know what it is to be oppressed and downtrodden. Pilgrim theology, in other words, goes with strength into the dark places that prosperous and privileged theologies can never reach.

In order to be properly equipped to be Christ's hands and feet, therefore, we as Christians must return to the basic theological premise that *we* are pilgrims and sojourners on this earth. We do not belong here; this is not our homeland. If we remember this and understand its implications, we will be able not only to empathize with the plight of the marginalized people groups of the world (like the Puerto Rican community in North Philadelphia), but also to be uniquely able to bring the gospel of true belonging, healing, and hope in Christ to the outcasts.

The church in North Philadelphia faces many trials and difficulties. Poverty, violence, racism, unemployment, inadequate housing, and the lack of quality healthcare and education are just a few of the external pressures churches face. These problems cause lasting damage to people, especially to children, in the form of sexual and domestic abuse and depression, and all the personal and communal cycles of pain that develop. Effective church help for the poor requires a basic but comprehensive understanding of the impact these areas have on the lives of the general population.

The growing church in this neighborhood is the only hope for bringing the *shalom* of God into the lives and homes of the people of North Philadelphia. It is the only living organism ordained by God to bring God's redeeming influence to all creation. Only the church can hold up the

---

34. Selby, *Grace*, 4.

promises of God as revealed in Scripture, doing battle for the soul and heart of its people until the kingdom of heaven is established on earth.

As such, the church must take an emphatic moral position against injustice: against the sexual abuse of children, spouses, or family members; the social structures that discriminate through race relations; economic disparity; police brutality; and the neglect of the physical environment. Through advocacy and organized community development,[35] the church has many avenues to be available to those who have been marginalized in these impoverished communities. The church will accomplish this as it seeks to emulate the supreme example of the Redeemer who died on the cross in order to reconcile an alienated world back to God, and to bring the kingdom of God and its righteousness to human society.

The manifestation of God's love for the people and community is incarnated through various ministries of mercy designed to help alleviate and comfort those who must live under the burden of poverty. The effects of poverty and exclusion serve as a daily reminder of the systemic forces that oppress the urban poor. The covenantal people of God will resist every force that rebels against the original plans of God for society, whether seen or unseen, and through the work of the church, we will see an overturning of the toxic patterns among the urban poor. In its obedience to God, the church will announce her prophetic voice to the world: that "the gates of hell shall not prevail" (Matt 16:18).

In the past two decades, we have experienced a radical change lived out in this community. The problems facing this new generation have become so sinister and complex that members of the previous generation truly struggle to comprehend the depth of these problems and the impact on their children and grandchildren. Once, Hispanic people of the Roman Catholic faith celebrated baptism, communion, and confession as sacraments; today among the young, very few bother. In their place we now find

35. Perkins, *Restoring At-Risk Communities*. According to Perkins, Christian community development must first begin with the aim of meeting spiritual needs. For this reason, the role of the church is crucial because Jesus mandated the church to "tear down the spiritual strongholds of hell," which have been established in our inner cities (Matt 16:13–19; 28:18–20). A recent example of a Christian community development effort involved close to twenty pastors and lay leaders. The group was organized by an indigenous pastor who encountered legal problems among his sheep. Some legal cases were unfairly handled by the office of the district attorney. After many meetings, the pastors, the district attorney, and her assistants took positive action to correct the problem. The district attorney appointed a liaison to handle any conflicts between law enforcement and her office.

the antithesis: instead of regeneration, degradation; instead of communion, alienation; and instead of confession, secrecy. Outright rebellion and boasting have replaced shame: in Spanish, *verguenza*, which implies accountability for personal moral behavior at the individual *and* at the community level. It encompasses consideration of how others perceive your character, not only one's internal struggle through emotion. "*No tiene verguenza,*" he has no shame, signifies a loss of conscience, and therefore a loss of moral pride. Once this has been displaced, there darkness and chaos follow—a darkness we now see about us.

Many people came to the Place of Refuge with this sense of a loss of integrity (their own, and that of their community). They presented to us their immediate problem with the hope that we might offer them relief, or answers to their suffering. In responding, we were keenly reminded that we must let the light of Christ shine in these dark places. At the Place of Refuge, we built an incarnational ministry as we shared the truth, love, and light of Christ—incarnational, not messianic—for we are but human instruments, a witness for the Lord, not the Savior ourselves.

In our counseling outreach, and in our equipping of lay counselors to become a capable body with the strength, knowledge, and courage to meet this darkness in their church and in their homes, we recognized that the healing of human suffering happens supernaturally. Even the most perfectly conceived ministry, social program, or outreach can only go so far. With this in mind, we followed our Redeemer: the light of the world, whose life and light can defeat darkness. We joined the ranks of those saints who came before us, following the light of Christ, and their memory too helped remind us of why we ministered to those in North Philadelphia:

> Paulinus . . . foreseeing the darkness ahead, decided to light a lamp and keep it burning in a Christian shrine . . . I should dearly love to [shine] . . . a lamp to signify that whatever the darkness, however profound the sense of lostness, the light of Christ's love and the clarity of his enlightenment still shine, and will continue to shine, for those who have eyes to see, a heart to love, and a soul to believe.[36]

We must take up the lantern. As I outline a biblical theology for a lay counseling outreach in the next chapter, we will take a closer look at the community we aim to build up in the light of Christ. The context is

---

36. Muggeridge, *Jesus Rediscovered*, 66.

vital as we explore a scriptural understanding and model, without failing to overlook the unique struggles that many experience in their daily lives.

Suffering can be confronted in meaningful ways, through professional therapy, medicine, and other avenues, but lay counseling represents Christian love in a unique form. It taps into the hidden treasures inside every believer. It is a way of investing our talents and skills in what the Lord has given us as believers to achieve:

> Each of us is matchless and should, for the good of the church and this community, be recognized as such and drawn upon to share our distinctiveness. We must be essentially what we are in the deepest calling of our natures and should be encouraged to express the gifts we have in order to contribute, share and participate in the growth of the community.[37]

Lay counseling strengthens people, telling them that life is worth living. In its simplest form, it allows God to enter in and to heal. It displaces the darkness of sin with the light of Christ, as the counselor speaks and utters the truth of our Lord—and the darkness does not overcome it. It grows, like music, like an inner harmony, like a symphony inside someone who once only looked upon the darkness, but now sees the risen Lord.

37. Hart, *Ear of the Heart*, 259.

2

Pilgrim Theology

THE ENCOUNTER WITH CHRIST ends in a day of glory. Suffering, as we find it among the children of God, can be made a holy work—transformative, incarnational, and transcendent—lifting us heavenward. In the time before Christ's coming, as we see with the children of Israel, God had set us apart in this world. Our trust (even through great suffering) brings us closer to God. To understand this journey, we must look first to its beginning and end. If we desire to appreciate it with all its worthy beauty, we must make many considerations, both historical and personal.

The journey of suffering and redemption has a recognizable, universal arc, and the story of both the Hebrew and Christian Scriptures is no different. We can see it through creation and the fall; Israel's journey in the wilderness to the promised land and later exile and suffering; the rebuilding of the temple; and finally, through the fulfillment of God's work through Christ and the establishment of the church on earth.

But God's word is a living word. It nourishes us not only with history but also in its message to the individual soul. This story arc adapts to single journeys, beginning in sin, in the dust and ash of the fall—and rising through suffering in Christ to glory.

The themes of suffering and glory can be traced throughout the lives of individuals and nations in the Bible. In the Hebrew Bible, we see them in the stories of the people of Israel and the prophets. The New Testament epistles offer wisdom; they encourage, they exhort us in practical ways not to stray from the path of Christ or follow false teachers; they inspire us to put our faith into action expressed in love. They are the testimonies of people who met Christ, and who wrote their letters to be read by the church of their day. Scripture also frames our current stories within its overarching grand story; in a real way, then, we can consider our stories the continuation of the unwritten section of the book of Acts. After all, we are living epistles.

This chapter, therefore, will address the theme of suffering by looking in Scripture at issues of alienation and the people of God in the company of suffering people and the world. My treatment of this theme splits into two distinct sections: the narrative in the Old Testament of God's preferential option for the marginalized—both within and outside the "chosen people"— and the Christ community's localizing of this narrative in the individual.

Arc of the Sacred Scriptures: From Creation to Christ

This first arc starts with creation, which has always been expressed in the creeds of the church. It is the first declaration in the Apostles' Creed: "I believe in God, the Father almighty, maker of heaven and earth."[1] These words stress the belief that God is the origin of all things, and that all things belong to and are subject to God.[2] The psalmist declared, "Blessed be his glorious name forever. May the whole earth be full of his glory" (Ps 72:19 KJV). Reflecting on these verses, I immediately think of God's pinnacle of creation, human beings.[3]

God placed Adam and Eve in Eden. It was rich and full of life, full of abundance in every respect, and also a refuge for the presence of God. Humanity fell away from God in rebellion, but God did not abandon us. We see immediately in Cain, who built the first city (Gen 4:17), the continuation of God's great design and purpose, despite the fall. Today, inarguably, our cities can be as tarnished as the perfect beauty of Eden. In our imperfect striving, we can yet see God's original design for humanity to give order and harmony to our surroundings.

God's purpose still remains true: to bring Eden into the midst of the city.

In Hebrew, the word for *city* or *town* is "iyr" (ריעה). It refers to any human settlement surrounded by a wall or fortification. Why is the city important for us? Why is it important to God? Why is it so central in

---

1. Episcopal Church, *Book of Common Prayer*, 53.

2. Berkhof, *Systematic Theology*. He asserts that creation is an act of a triune God, p. 129.

3. Murray, *Collected Writings*, 3–8. Murray outlines the distinctiveness found in humans, primarily that the identity of humans consists in the image and likeness of God.

Scripture? In Jer 29:7, the Lord commanded that the exiled Jews seek the peace of the city of their captivity. In Paul's travels, and in his letters, it is on behalf of the cities of Asia Minor and Greece that he pours himself out. In the eschatological consummation of Christ revealed in the book of Revelation, the city is the setting of the New Jerusalem—the consummation of God's project beginning with Eden. It is the joy of the whole earth in Ps 48:2, where God is glorified through a holy nation, a holy people. Hence, biblically, the city is a cosmopolitan place where people live together in community, have businesses, and enjoy the strengths of their cultures. In both the Old and New Testaments, portrayals of cities show a place where the people of God seek the common good for all who live there.

For a long time, the city has been (and must still be) the epicenter of missions. As noted in the Jer 29 passage, Jehovah instructed the people to seek the peace of the city while in exile in Babylon. Like many today who find themselves aliens or illegal immigrants—and some legal immigrants, too—the mandate holds the same power: those who fear God must build the communities around themselves.

Nowhere is this alienation, this endless exile, more fiercely felt than among the poor. They feel this many-layered exile not only in the pinch of geographic displacement, but in the economic and the social sphere as well. And yet, even in exile, the gospel teaches us our duty to the surrounding society and to each other.

Creation is on vibrant display in the city. Any visitor to my own community of North Philadelphia will be surprised by the dynamic flow of life here; although the people experience the universal alienation and brokenness that all humans face, the residual echoes of God's creation can be seen in the entrepreneurial spirit of the small shop owners, the cultural centers, the gifts and talents used in various community projects, the ethnic diversity among the people, and in the many churches representing various Protestant denominations and Roman Catholic traditions. Many of the evangelical churches are small storefront Pentecostal congregations, but they participate in significant outreach to the local community, especially in reaching out to drug users. Among the Catholic churches, many are socially active, especially when it comes to helping local children. These reflect God's creation and original patterns,[4] and—although marred by the effects

---

4. Berkhof, *Systematic*, 129. "The work of creation was not divided among the three persons, but the whole work, though from different aspects, is ascribed to each one of the persons." The principle here is that, while humans may maintain their independence, they can also work together in creative ways reflecting on the Trinity.

of the fall—they are still good and true.[5] They represent the remnants of God's cultural task of building a kingdom on earth through multiplication and dominion over all of creation. People work as co-creators, deriving their abilities from God. They have been endowed with intelligence analogous to that of God,[6] an imaginative ability that enables them to fulfill the cultural mandate of fruitfulness and multiplication established by God at creation (Gen 1:28).

God commanded Adam to work the land. This call continues to rule in our hearts, despite the fall. Our design as humans includes the capacity to have dominion over "creation," whether that creation is in the city or in paradise. With our work, we display the desire to use nascent abilities for income, which provides sustenance for our loved ones and dependents. North Philadelphia no longer holds many manufacturing factories, as was once the case.[7] Now, only small private businesses tell of the community and personal work ethic: mechanic repair shops, beauty salons, medical centers, technological stores, grocery mini markets, department stores, and restaurants specializing in Spanish cuisine.

The city's cultural life emerges in educational centers, in theaters and museums, and in the agencies and public schools that work to ensure the passing of ideas and cultural inheritance to the next generation. All of these things are woven together in a glorious tapestry, testifying to the dignity of work and the wealth of creative gifts endowed to humanity by God the Creator.

Like the diversity in the animal kingdom we enjoy at the zoo or in the wild, God has graciously created beautiful and diverse human beings. Their appearance, body type, language, customs, traditions, food, emotional expression, and intellectual patterns are as varied as the plants in my home country, Puerto Rico. Yet these differences do not override basic human commonalities. Life's central questions and answers are the same for all people, as anthropologist Charles Kraft writes, "The diverse cultures of the world's people constitute just so many answers to essentially the same sets of questions posed by human situations."[8] In the first chapter of Genesis,

5. Van Til, *Dilemma*, 35.

6. Van Til, *Dilemma*, 11. He points out that in non-Christian theorizing, men reason univocally, while in Christianity, men reason analogically. God and man, he argues, must be thought of as correlative to one another.

7. Adams et al., *Philadelphia Neighborhoods*, 20–24.

8. Kraft, *Anthropology*, 119.

God creates this diversity and, upon its completion, declares it good. Differences between cultures are actually indicative of how similar we are to God and each other, rather than hostile or alien, because our creativity in designing cultural patterns is derivative of God's creative nature.[9] While in the suburbs, overt cultural patterns can be harder to see, in the city, the diversity is evident—and thriving.

Finally, human creation explodes in the central vibrancy of personality and spirit. Within the Hispanic community in North Philadelphia, I find some of the most colorful souls. The inquisitive children, asking for attention, seeking interaction; the young Latinas who express their sexuality and beauty; the sociable and outgoing *jovenes* (young guys) hanging out fixing their cars and motorcycles; the youthful women on the sidewalks, lugging several children and smiling in greeting; and the laughing men in social clubs and restaurants (and the clinic!)—all speak of the joy of being alive and celebrating life.

Spirituality abounds. Deep within every life, there lies a heart that fervently awaits something beyond its reach, something that it intuitively senses will bring ultimate satisfaction. People coming to the Place of Refuge often struggle to express this sense, however vague, that they *know* there is something better out there for them. When this "something" remains unfulfilled, disappointment and despair often follow.

Some, however, remain open to the possibility that, perhaps, the "something" is God. Whether the soul understands that longing or not, it is a created part of their identities and cannot be wholly ignored. Their desire for good things is noticeably persistent and wonderfully alive: whether as a desire for work, for personal growth in education, for creativity through artistic means, or for strong interpersonal relationships. All of these desires come from and connect us back to God. As counselors, we have the privilege of helping connect people's longings to God.

The Fall

The biblical narrative of Adam and Eve reveals that they disobeyed God, and one serious ramification for their disobedience was to experience a change in their relationship with God, with each other, and with their environment. In the first few chapters of Genesis, the original scene of Eden shows God walking with Adam and Eve in the cool of the day, symbolizing

9. Kraft, *Anthropology*, 118.

the intended communion between God and humanity in the ages to come. When they disobeyed, God acted as the sovereign judge of the created universe; all parties involved received their due penalty, including Satan, the serpent. The result, according to this ancient tale, was their exile from Eden and therefore from that direct, easy communion with God—indicating the distance humans feel between themselves and the divine. Life would continue for Adam and Eve, but increased in difficulty. Suffering—physically, through the labor of the fields and childbirth; emotionally and psychologically, through wrongly placed desire and unsettled power dynamics; and spiritually, through felt-alienation from God—would become the new norm. Even their interaction with the earth worsened. The multi-layered dynamics in their relationship to each other, to God, and to their surroundings catastrophically changed.

This passage teaches a terrifying truth about the reality of the fall: sin causes death to the soul of a human being. And so the question is, *What can we expect a dead soul to produce?* In its natural state, it produces works of evil, and as a consequence, it teaches us that we are children of wrath (Eph 2:7b). This is a hard truth to process, especially in American society, because our current cultural philosophy teaches the opposite: that people are basically good. But the truth of God must stand.

Several years ago, I walked into a local Spanish restaurant to purchase lunch. The owner, doubling as waitress, was a friendly woman and, because I was a regular customer, shared some of her concerns regarding the spiritual condition of many in our community. Since the discussion turned to infant baptism and what she described as "preparation for the Holy Communion," I knew she practiced the Roman Catholic faith. She told me that the people in the community rarely practice these two sacred Catholic ordinances, both of which have, historically, been integral parts of Puerto Rican culture. In her view, this was a real sign of spiritual disintegration among her people.

This reminded me of the encounter Jesus had with the Samaritan woman in John 4. Her life as a woman was already complicated and precarious, as evidenced in part by her relational history, but it was compounded by her status as a racial outcast whose form of the faith of Yahweh was considered bastardized by Jesus' people.

In the course of their conversation, Jesus revealed himself to her as the Messiah—the possessor of the water of life—and she believed him.[10] From

---

10. The Samaritan woman was part Jewish and part Assyrian. As such, she understood

that point on, she no longer lived in alienation from her spiritual self. Like the Samaritan woman, many of the people I counsel—particularly in the Hispanic community—have religious inclinations and beloved traditions, but no in-depth knowledge of God. The hallmark of the fall in their lives is found in their broken identities; these are created based on lesser things, rather than discovering their full, true selves as children of God. As Oswald Chambers famously wrote: "The good is always the enemy of the best."[11] Normal desires for love and human relationships are naturally good things to want, but when these desires rule our hearts, they become a powerful foe.

Spiritual alienation is manifested in various aspects of a person's life. Like the Samaritan woman, their place in the world is often defined by the romantic alliances they have developed with different people through the years. Since their relationship with God—like Adam and Eve—is broken, they are uncomfortable being alone for periods at a time; they find it hard, if not impossible, to live without romantic intimacy.

Yet Eph 2 compels us to evaluate this position. It clearly puts the responsibility where it belongs: according to Paul, it is sin that causes the soul to die, and consequently, the death inside of us perpetuates itself in unfruitful works. "A state of sin," writes Matthew Henry,

> is a state of conformity to this world. Wicked men are slaves to Satan. Satan is that author of the proud carnal disposition which there is in ungodly men; he rules in the hearts of men. From Scripture, it is clear, that whether man hath been most prone to sensual or to spiritual wickedness, all men, being naturally children of disobedience, are also by nature children of God.[12]

How, then, does humanity go from being a child of disobedience to becoming a child of God? We do not return to Eden, to innocence, but are given a new regenerate life, where, before a holy, living God, we sit at the right hand. According to Paul in Ephesians, "Like the rest, we were by nature deserving of wrath. But because of his great love for us, God, who is rich in mercy, made us alive with Christ even when we were dead in transgressions—it is by grace you have been saved" (Eph 2:3b–5 NIV).

---

the spiritual significance of the Jewish prophecy of the coming Messiah as well as the impact that this Messiah would have on the people in her community. Jesus stayed with the Samaritans for two days. Interestingly, this was the first time Jesus revealed that he was the Messiah.

11. Chambers, *My Utmost*, 25.

12. Henry, "Ephesians 2."

Grace, or God's unmerited favor, as John Leonard defines it,[13] brings life to the dead and healing in places that seemed broken beyond repair. As Henry proclaims, "None can from Scripture abuse this doctrine, or accuse it of any tendency to evil. All who do so are without excuse."[14]

Israel in the Wilderness: Sacrifice, Wandering, and Exile

In the garden, Adam and Eve set the pattern with their disobedience. The Bible's continuing narrative arc shows rebellion against God growing and repeating with time. In Noah's generation, humanity had descended into such wickedness that God sent the flood. Familial relationships betray the strain of sin, as seen in Jacob and Esau, Joseph and his brothers, and Miriam and Aaron's rebellion against Moses. The judges and prophets bear testimony to the faithlessness and treachery of Israel, and their constant failure to rise to God's standard of righteousness or fulfill their duty to bring light to the world.

The sin so prevalent among God's people must be dealt with somehow.

Unclean, they feared they could not stand in God's presence with the ease that Adam and Eve once had, walking with God in Eden. And so the Lord reached out to the people, showing his eternal desire to make a way for them to come near. God did this with the Israelites through the building of the tabernacle and the giving of the law.

The motif of the tabernacle (and later, the temple) as illustrated in Leviticus is vitally important. It points to the significance of the tabernacle as foreshadowing the temple—and the spiritual "templehood"—of Christ and the Christian believer. In his book *The Shadow of Christ in the Law of Moses*, Vern Poythress tells us that just as the true dwelling place of God is in heaven, so the tabernacle is the dwelling place of God on earth.[15] We must say that the earthly tabernacle foreshadowed the work of the Messiah.

The shadow, in this sense, is inferior to the reality; the earthly tabernacle could never equal the majestic splendor of our God in heaven. The shadow, in other words, is not in itself the reality, but rather points to Christ, the ultimate reality. All things in the Hebrew Bible, read through a New Testament lens, center on the Messiah.

13. Leonard, "Celebrating Grace."
14. Henry, "Ephesians 2."
15. Poythress, *Shadow*. See Ex 29:45; Heb 8:5, 9:24.

The entire book of Leviticus illustrates the obligation of purity as exemplified in the levitical laws. We must view Leviticus in connection with the revelation of God in the book of Exodus, where we read of Moses' personal encounter with God on Mt. Sinai. On the mountaintop, Moses received instructions from God concerning the construction of the tabernacle (Ex 24:15–18; 26:30), which, in the Hebrew Bible, both symbolized and physically *was* God's dwelling with Israel, but to the New Testament writers also symbolized Christ and the salvation he offers to humanity.

As the narrative in Exodus reveals, and in an echo of Adam and Eve's choice in Eden, the idolatrous inclination of the Israelites (as seen in the worship of the golden calf in Ex 32) threatened to abnegate God's purposes to dwell with them. Moses, in his compassionate attempt to spare them from God's anger, offered himself as a substitute for their sins, but God did not accept this offer. The sacrifices outlined in Leviticus underscore the validity of substitution for the remissions of sins, pointing to the divine substitutionary sacrifice of Christ as the Lamb of God.

The immediate context of Lev 19:2 plunges us into the reality of a fully constructed tabernacle wherein God came down in a great cloud. Yet the problem of sin among God's people continued. The entire contents of Leviticus, in fact, address this ongoing problem. The sacrifices God established for the Israelites were inherently redemptive in nature, in that they served to cleanse the people and the tabernacle from the defilement of sin.

The role of the priest who would intercede on behalf of the Israelites was incredibly significant and naturally has many points of connection with Christ. In this chapter, we focus our attention on those passages that best crystalize Christ's priestly and sacrificial acts, his submission to his messianic woes, and his example and union with us to bring redemption, as the fulcrum of holiness.

The priestly role and the various sacrifices made for the cleansing of sin prefigure the final sacrifice of Christ. Poythress explains that where the "sin offering makes atonement for specific sins" for the worshiper, the burnt offering makes "atonement for sinfulness generally."[16]

In the burnt offering ritual, there existed an intimate association between the worshipper and the sacrificial animal, in which the worshipper recognized the animal's fate as symbiotic with her own. Traditionally, the worshiper would lay her hand on its head while its blood spilled on the altar, since without this blood, she could have no relationship with God. The

---

16. Poythress, *Shadow*, 48.

preparing and burning of the animal was done in an orderly and elaborate manner by the priest.

In general, the people had to separate themselves from uncleanness—they could not survive unless they learned to respect the holiness of God and practiced holiness amongst themselves. This was especially important in order to approach the tabernacle (Num 8:10).

Poythress states that "the law was the instrument and expression for God's kingly rule over Israel."[17] In the Scriptures, these Hebrew laws not only record God's revelation of a divine order of society, but also seek to establish a unique nation: a truly "chosen people." The book of Leviticus, therefore, anticipates the future status of Israel as God's chosen people and—in a broader sense—the inclusion of Gentiles among God's people, as they are united through God's atonement of sins.

Thus, keeping in mind the origin of these laws and recognizing their historical context, we come to understand them as a reflection of their times. As already mentioned, these laws were implemented to serve as God's supreme guiding rules for the people of Israel. The concept of levitical purity, as recorded in Numbers, has its roots in the idea of Jehovah as the supreme, holy God (Num 11:44, 20:24–26), and of the people of Israel as a kingdom of priests (Ex 19:6). We can perceive at this point the intimate connection of the people of Israel with the holiness of their king. In his hermeneutical analysis, however, Poythress concludes that the difference in the types of sacrifices is largely one of degree.[18] The important thing, says Poythress, is that the sacrifices and the variety found in them "emphasize different aspects in the process of communion with God."[19] Yet, most importantly, Poythress offers this final interpretation of the sacrificial system:

> All of these aspects are combined fully in the sacrifice of Jesus Christ on the cross. Christ bore the punishment for our sins (1 Peter 2:24; Isaiah 53:5). Thus He is the final sin offering. Christ was wholly consecrated to God. He suffered death and destruction for sin, and also brings about our death to sin (Romans 6:2–7). Thus He is the final grain offering. Christ now offers us His flesh to eat (John 6:54–58). By partaking of His flesh and blood we have eternal life, we have communion with the Father, and we are

17. Poythress, *Shadow*, 76.

18. Poythress, *Shadow*, 43.

19. Poythress, *Shadow*, 49.

transformed into Christ's image (2 Corinthians 3:18). Thus Christ is the final fellowship offering.[20]

We can see Christ's conclusive, complete offering fulfilling the levitical specifications by comparing Christ to the prior sacrificial system just described. We can see the mark of that which was "incomplete and temporary" in the fact that the sacrifices were a daily ritual; also, under the prior covenant, the priest brought the sacrifice into the sanctuary: both in direct contrast to the sacrifice of Christ. Not only was his a "once for all" sacrifice (Heb 9:25—10:18), but Christ offered himself, not another's life. In other words, the High Priest *was* the perfect, unblemished sacrifice.[21]

The prophets spoke in the dispensation of waiting for the Messiah. They believed as we believe, but his coming had not yet come to pass. In the voice of the prophets—such as Moses, Elijah, Ezra, Jeremiah, and Isaiah—we hear the cry of the city; we hear God calling Israel to return. And their cries to God in response hold both joy and pain. In their wilderness wanderings before coming into the promised land, and later, in their repeated experiences of exile among the nations, the people of God knew great suffering.

People today, as with the Israelites, often wander in the wilderness. This is true especially of those isolated outside of the church, but it also holds true in the lives of suffering believers within the church. Even in their wilderness, they want God and crave divine guidance. They feel the reality of separation from God and the sting of suffering. Their need for the priest and for sacrifice—for Christ—remains just as strong now as then. And in God's careful instruction to the people, we can see that there is a longing to make a way for the people to come to God, to learn how to relate to the divine holiness, and ultimately to become holy themselves. If we care about God, this must be our work as well.

As Israel passed through the wilderness, their time there was a preparation to live again in the presence of God—in the promised land. We might characterize the wilderness as the absence of the idyllic state—except that the presence of God was with them. Without it, they would not have been capable of walking in God's ways.

But even in the promised land, the people went astray. The Lord knew that sin and death waited for them in disobedience. Once again, to remain true to the covenant, God sent them prophets, who pointed the people

---

20. Poythress, *Shadow*, 49.

21. Snodgrass, "He Offered Up," 567.

back, and allowed the construction of the temple as a permanent reminder of God's presence. The material world of the promised land is the outward manifestation, or the reflection of the inward spiritual condition, of God's people. Sin and darkness within them became evident in the land—barren when their disobedience exiled them, and fruitful when repentance brought them back.

Israel, like her first parents, went through rebellion and exile, being called again to regain her right relation to God as a pilgrim people, writing psalms in a strange land. Yet God did not intend Canaan as their final home: "Instead, they were longing for a better country—a heavenly one. Therefore God is not ashamed to be called their God, for he has prepared a city for them" (Heb 11:16 NIV). So too do we seek out God's face, for ours is a pilgrim God.

The Arc of the Sacred Scriptures: The Coming of Christ

The temple of Herod, with its ornate golden vine cutting into the stones,[22] points back to Israel, called God's vine, and the repeated images of the people of God sitting each under their own vines and fig trees in peace (Zech 3:10; Mic 4:4). The New Testament retains this beautiful metaphor with Christ as the true vine, and us sitting with him in the last feast. In Christ's coming, we see the final destruction of the temple, now rendered obsolete. In the incarnation, Christ creates a new people: the church, made now of both Jews and Greeks, those from every nation and tongue. The church of Christ emerges from the chosen remnant, sealed with the Holy Spirit. They worship God, not in a temple built with stone, but rather in spirit and truth. Christians are called to model Christ and join him in pilgrimage. He calls women and men to partake with him, to sit and drink and eat, and then to pick up their walking sticks: paradise awaits.

Rebuilding the Temple

Through the authority and sacrifice of Christ, God took the holiness from the temple and gave it to every believer. The humility and meekness of this act carries all grace and challenges every witness to answer: respond according to what you have heard, for you will be judged. In closeness to

22. Josephus, *Works*.

God through union with Christ, we experience our salvation—not by good deeds, but by our childlike faith that believes the truth of God. In the fulfillment of our calling, it is God's way, truth, and life that we must follow.

Those who live in poverty confront real hardship in everyday life, yet nothing can compare with the spiritual poverty depicted in Eph 2. Paul writes about a death that is inextricably connected to trespasses and sins, about a death to those who walk according to the course of this world, to the prince of the power of the air, to the spirit that is now working in the children of disobedience. This is the depiction of a soul that is dead. In the urban setting, the negative accumulation of stress can be summed in the prevalence of crime, money, guns, drugs, and a growing homelessness. Paul describes such a person in Eph 2:3 (KJV), a person who lives "in the lust of the flesh, fulfilling the desires of the flesh and of the mind," and who is "by nature [a child] of wrath . . ." But despite this, God pursues this very person in that spiritually dark place. In fact, this is precisely where Christ's work of redemption has such power. Christ came, after all, to save the sinner—for the sick, not the healthy, are the ones who need a doctor.

Pilgrim Theology

In Jas 1:1 and 1 Pet 1:1, Christians are portrayed as aliens in this world. We are to have our eyes on our true citizenship, which is in heaven. Moses challenged the Israelites to choose whether they would follow God or the gods of the nations, choosing life or death: they could not choose both (Deut 30:19–20). We are sent to the places of the world as sojourners or pilgrims to build the kingdom of God on earth, to get ourselves personally involved in the lives of people. In 1 Pet 2:11–12, we get a sense of what this looks like to God. Notice what we read: believers are to do good deeds and glorify God in the midst of those who are spiritually alienated from God. We are ambassadors for Christ, speaking of his hope.

The world is the setting of redemption where the gospel has been proclaimed. Therefore, we have the challenging commission to interact in this world while holding loosely to worldly things. One cannot be friends with both God and the world: "Don't you know that friendship with the world means enmity against God? Therefore, anyone who chooses to be a friend of the world becomes an enemy of God" (Jas 4:4 NIV).

Scripture takes the notion of this commission to a higher level by introducing what scholars call a *pilgrim theology*. This theology appears in many of the New Testament writings, as well as in the writings of the early church. Benjamin Dunning notes related "resident-alien topos" found in other ancient texts: terms such as *paroikos* ("resident alien"), *xenos* ("stranger-foreigner"), *parepidemos* ("sojourner"), and *politeia* ("citizenship"), all used to express "what it meant for them to be Christian," especially as a marginalized minority within the dominance of secular Roman culture.[23] These texts are plentiful in Scripture and elsewhere in early Christian texts, and because of this, an exhaustive treatment of them is outside the scope of this book. Instead, for our purposes, we will examine the formation of pilgrim theology in the book of 1 Peter.

What we find in 1 Peter is something different from the writings of the prophets—for Christ has come. As George Eldon Ladd has it, "The death of Christ is not merely an event that promises an eschatological salvation; it is itself the object of messianic prophecy. The eschatological glory is inseparably related to the sufferings of Christ."[24]

Peter, in his writing to the scattered churches of the provinces of Asia, understands that Christ's coming to the world was the fulfillment of messianic prophecy.[25] He is a witness to the resurrection, regarding it "as the beginning of the eschatological (messianic) era."[26] In light of this new era, he offers his framework for the life of the believer in the midst of a troubling world.

In order to appreciate the value of the essential themes of 1 Peter (and especially, for our purposes, of the epistle's theme of Christians as aliens in the world), we must first understand this epistle in its full historical context. The principal themes of 1 Peter are holiness, submission, and suffering.

In his article, "Honorable Conduct Among the Gentiles," Earl J. Richard notes that 1 Peter begins with societal and religious concerns regarding Christian living in a worldly environment, when faced with many trials.[27] Peter describes the audience as both of the "dispersion" (1:1) and as "aliens and exiles" (2:11). They may have been either Jewish converts from the Diaspora, or (more likely) Gentile converts to Christianity.

23. Dunning, *Aliens*, 1.

24. Ladd, *Theology*, 595.

25. Richard, "Honorable Conduct," 412. The biblical author claims that he is "Peter, an apostle of Jesus Christ," but many modern scholars argue for pseudonymity. For the sake of brevity, however, I use Peter's name to reference this author, whatever his actual identity might have been.

26. Ladd, *Theology*, 595.

27. Richard, "Honorable," 413.

In either case, the crucial fact is that they lived as Christians among non-Christians. By use of the term *dispersion* or "elect exiles of the diaspora" (1:1), he reminds them that they are not living in a utopian society but among other fallen human beings, within a community of fellow believers sharing the same "religious character."[28] His other phrase, "aliens and exiles" (2:11), begins "a lengthy social code on behavior toward outsiders and insiders, involving political and social concerns."[29] The code made it clear that Christians, despite their separate nature, had civil, political, and neighborly duties to the rest of society (one might call this the "civic duty" aspect of pilgrim theology).

This civic duty is not limited to tax-paying and other responsibilities to one's governing institutions. Richard believes that the expression found in 2:13, "Be subject for the Lord's sake to every human institution," does not satisfactorily reflect the meaning of the original Greek: the phrase *every human institution* should more properly be translated *every human individual*. This interpretation leads to a more satisfactory reading of 2:17 to "honor everyone. Love the brotherhood. Fear God. Honor the emperor." Richard concludes, "Basic then to 1 Peter's social thought is the claim . . . that all human creatures are owed honor . . . [Christians are to] live responsibly in society, for they are to 'recognize their duty toward' other humans. Indeed, this duty is characterized in the same pericope as 'honoring everyone.'"[30] Thus, a pilgrim theology grounds its instructions on living in mainstream society in the firm, biblical understanding that Christians owe honorable conduct toward the non-Christians with whom they live.

The reason Peter needed to detail such a social code within his treatment of pilgrim theology was "the result of hostility, harassment, and social, unofficial ostracism on the part of the general populace."[31] Christians are asked, in the face of such trials, to conduct themselves with self-control and long-suffering. They are to exemplify a dignity that puts them above the insults and abuses inflicted upon them simply because they are "other." They ought to imitate Christ explicitly in the context of suffering.

Within this framework, Peter introduces the state of affairs in the world and what life will be like for the Christian. He asserts that the world remains an evil place where "[y]our enemy the devil prowls around like

28. Richard, "Honorable," 417.
29. Richard, "Honorable," 417.
30. Richard, "Honorable," 417, 419.
31. Richard, "Honorable," 414.

a roaring lion looking for someone to devour" (1 Pet 5:8b NIV). Clearly, the Christian life will have suffering and persecution. Salvation will bring a new hope as Christians walk in the newness of life: "In his great mercy he has given us new birth into a living hope" (1 Pet 1:3b NIV), and Peter regards this hope highly, as a strengthening influence in the world.

As Christians, we are God's children, redeemed by the death and resurrection of Jesus Christ. This knowledge imprints upon our souls that we must imitate Christ in the midst of trials—indeed, in all of life—and this is exactly what Peter calls his audience to do. The example God sets before Christians to follow is not Jesus as Messiah, but Jesus as sufferer.

But it is not only suffering in which we imitate Christ, even when our suffering feels innocent or unmerited, like his. We also participate in his subsequent glory, described as "an inheritance that can never perish, spoil, or fade" (1 Pet 1:4a NIV). The entire process of suffering, then, hinges on the doctrine of soteriology. The saving mission of the Christ event, stressed in 1 Peter, is the gift of new life as the source of strength and solidarity for the community of believers.[32]

Clearly, the group of believers reading 1 Peter faced persecution and suffering from their unbelieving neighbors. Peter's model for honorable conduct—the model that will help us to make a bridge between the church and non-believers—has its roots in a shared experience of marginalization. As such, it is deeply comparable to the experiences of a minority population situated in the wider community, feeling every day that they are the "other." The God of Scripture is nearest to those who suffer.

Suffering Servants

To carry this thought further, Orlando Costas comments on Isa 53, "The Suffering Servant situates the cross on the side of the poor and the afflicted, the sick and the oppressed . . . Jesus takes the form of a slave in his incarnation, becoming totally identified with humanity in its lowest form."[33] Nevertheless, suffering as a given in Christ's life and in the life of the believer poses significant difficulty for most of us. No other chapter in Scripture, perhaps, offers such a challenge as does Col 1:24–29:

32. Richard, "Honorable," 416.
33. Costas, *Christ*, 7.

> Now I rejoice in my sufferings for your sake, and in my flesh I am filling up what is lacking in Christ's afflictions for the sake of his body, that is, the church, of which I became a minister according to the stewardship from God that was given to me for you, to make the word of God fully known, the mystery hidden for ages and generations but now revealed to his saints. To them God chose to make known how great among the Gentiles are the riches of the glory of this mystery, which is Christ in you, the hope of glory. Him we proclaim, warning everyone and teaching everyone with all wisdom, that we may present everyone mature in Christ. For this I toil, struggling with all his energy that he powerfully works within me.

Here, as elsewhere in the Scriptures, we are told to rejoice in our suffering; we are to fill in that which is lacking in Christ's affliction for the sake of the church. In his essay on this passage, Watkins expresses what many of us may privately say upon reading such words: "Has the apostle Paul gone too far?"[34]

Of course the answer is no. There is nothing lacking in Christ's atonement; he did it all. For Paul, the "theology of suffering and servanthood . . . are inseparable from union with Christ."[35] Paul is a living example of a sufferer: as in Acts 9:15–16, where Paul was appointed to carry the gospel before the Israelites and Gentiles and, as was prophesied, would suffer for Christ's name's sake.

In like fashion, Christ, as predicted in Isa 53, would play the role of the suffering servant for the sake of humanity. However, Watkins further notes that Isaiah's prophecy here was not completely fulfilled by Christ, but passed to the church after Pentecost. After all, Jesus' living ministry was primarily to the nation of Israel and not to Gentiles. When Gentiles began coming to Christ, his earthly ministry drew to an end as the cross grew ever closer (John 12:20–26). It would be Christ's followers and disciples— indeed, the church—who would proclaim the gospel to all nations through the pouring out of the Holy Spirit (Matt 18:28–30; Acts 1:6–8).

In this sense, therefore, when Paul begins to preach to the Gentiles and suffers for it, he fills in the sufferings of Christ. He becomes both the proclaimer of the gospel as well as the poster child of suffering, for the cause of Christ. This is a great mystery, but it connects him to the suffering Christ and connects the people of God to the suffering Messiah.[36] "The gospel

---

34. Watkins, "Filling Up," 570.

35. Watkins, "Filling Up," 572.

36. Watkins, "Filling Up," 572–74.

proclaimed by his lips is the gospel evidenced in his life. It is his reference point for all things. It is not only his lens for understanding his trials, but his consolation in the midst of them."[37] This explains the apostle's joy: that in his sufferings, he was reflecting the acknowledgement that Christ suffered for him, considering it a privilege. As Christians, we will suffer and be persecuted for Christ's sake. If the master suffers, so will the servant (2 Tim 3:12).

In that suffering, however, we are not without God's presence. God shares with us in our suffering as we share in Christ's. How does God demonstrate this presence? One way God often transforms our suffering is through compassion. As Elizabeth Conde-Frazier notes,

> The origin of the word *compassion* is from the words *cum patior*, which means to suffer with, to undergo with. It connotes solidarity. Compassion works from a place of strength of mutuality. It means participating in the suffering of another from a strength born of awareness of shared weakness. It is this sense of shared weakness that distinguishes compassion from pity.[38]

And so, as Conde-Frazier quotes Henry, "Grace in the soul is a new life in the soul. A regenerated sinner becomes a living soul; he lives a life of holiness, being born of God. He lives, being delivered from the guilt of sin, by pardoning and justifying grace."[39] Accepting and using suffering for God's good purposes, in this context, is made possible by this great grace. Given through the atonement of Jesus Christ, this grace raises us all above the earth, above what our natural state would be: above the spiritual, psychological, personal, and environmental brokenness brought about by the fall. God's grace is a gift, produced by the Holy Spirit.

Atonement and Redemption: The Model for Believers

The incarnation of Christ fulfilled the teaching of John 1:14, "The Word became flesh and dwelt among us," which epitomized the promise that God would dwell among humans, as was clearly intended from the first establishing of God's tabernacle with God's covenant people, the Israelites. This promise will reach its eschatological fulfillment in the New Jerusalem: "And I heard a loud voice from the throne saying, 'Behold, the dwelling place of

37. Watkins, "Filling Up," 574.

38. Conde-Frazier, "Spirituality," 74.

39. Conde-Frazier, "Spirituality," 74.

God is with man. He will dwell with them, and they will be his people, and God himself will be with them as their God'" (Rev 21:3).

The atonement of Christ is the provision of God's love for a spiritually alienated humanity.[40] God cannot, however, simply overlook defiance to divine majesty as expressed through a counterfeit spirituality: finding means of spiritual authority based on religious customs and traditions, or in following after false gods. Puerto Rican culture, while expressing a shadow of God's original intent for communal living, in actuality lives in alienation.

Bright spots exist, however, for those who are seeking redemption. Rom 3:25–26 (NIV) confirms,

> God presented Christ as a sacrifice of atonement, through the shedding of his blood—to be received by faith. He did this to demonstrate his righteousness, because in his forbearance he had left the sins committed beforehand unpunished—he did it to demonstrate his righteousness at the present time, so as to be just and the one who justifies those who have faith in Jesus.

The work of Christ in life and death satisfies what humans have understood as the inscrutable justice of God, and the hope for all people—and my community of North Philadelphia—rests on this one fact: God's love as expressed to them on Calvary is the only true source of redemption, offering an open door to the divine heart for a life of eternal reconciliation and *shalom*.

Scripture offers many pictures of this redemption process. Among these pictures that shed light into the nature of redemption is Ezek 37:1–6. In this passage, we go from the death of the soul, which sin produces in all of us, to the resurrection of the soul, which the grace of God produces in those who experience regeneration. Ezekiel's vision of the valley of the dry bones points to the power of God to resurrect "our souls from death of sin to the life of righteousness, to a holy, heavenly, spiritual, and divine life, by the power of divine grace going along with the word of Christ, in John 5:24–25."[41] As seen in this passage, the dead soul moves from the deplorable condition of dead, dry bones to breath and life and the wonderful effect of God's immeasurable grace.

Then, too, Christ gives the story of the prodigal son as an image of deadness turned to life, the lost soul experiencing resurrection. In his sermon on this parable, John Leonard focuses on the grace evident in the

---

40. Murray, *Collected Writings*, 145.

41. Henry, "Ezekiel 37."

story. It is transformational, but it also challenges the basic assumptions we have about God and ourselves—about who we are, and about who God is. We measure ourselves by the wrong standard; in truth, God is the one to whom we must look.

In Leonard's words, "The real tragedy of our lives is that we do not reach the full potential God has created us for."[42] This tragedy is evidenced by the experience of the young brother in the prodigal son story. He leaves his family and winds up bankrupt, spiritually and emotionally alienated from his father and older brother. In contrast, his older brother is also in the barnyard feeding pigs. Both were dead, lives broken by this felt-lack. Both needed grace. "We can never make up for the lack in our own selves,"[43] says Leonard. This is what makes grace so hard to accept. We cannot believe that God, as the father in the story, robes us, feeds us, throws a celebration on our behalf, and becomes ecstatic when we return home to him—whether we journeyed far or stood, angry and aloof, in the other room. Yet it is only in our relationship with God and through God's unmerited favor, poured gratuitously on all things, that we live.

The redemption of Christ brings newness of life[44] and prescribes principles for the conducting of a whole, fruitful life. As the adopted offspring of the living God, a stronger identity forms; the individual's worth no longer resides in the lesser things of culturally defined religion, romantic liaisons, employment status or wealth, national pride, or acceptable physical standards of beauty and sexuality.

Growth and maturation take place within, shaping a new character. "The set of interdependent traits," writes Roberts, "including kindness, humility, patience, gratitude, love, faith, hope, and wisdom from above, binds everything together in perfect harmony."[45] The gospel creates a fresh psychology for the inner life, and a rejuvenated personality is resurrected. In the intimacy of communion with the triune God, the alienated and oppressed—the hounded and displaced—all find a powerful and lasting identity in God's eyes.

The gospel of Christ directly impacts the definition of male and female gender roles, through which people experience progressive transformation into the image of Christ. It overturns the *machismo/marianismo* cultural

42. Leonard, "Celebrating Grace."

43. Leonard, "Celebrating Grace."

44. Volf, *After Our Likeness*, 81–82.

45. Roberts, "Philosophy."

paradigm. While mysterious psychological and spiritual differences between men and women exist according to God's design, both genders are called to a life of holiness and service to others. Both are to reach full maturity as they become integrated into the body of Christ in their local congregations and community.

A sanctified man is a lover of God first. Echoing Christ's self-emptying life and death, he spends his God-derived power loving those around him well, expending himself for the life of the world around him, exhibiting moral integrity and self-control.

Likewise, a holy woman develops her love of God deeply. Her faith becomes the bedrock of her existence, the source from which balance, wholeness, and peace are accessible to her. She is not confined to either (as we examined in chapter 1) the *mariana* or the *hembrista* role, but learns to follow the Holy Spirit's inward guidance rather than that of her culture's expectations. She learns to set boundaries, refuses to accept abuse, and discovers the liberating power of God manifested in her life through both softness and strength.

The best image I have seen of a woman achieving this balance is the wife of a local pastor. She holds a master's degree and has raised two children, and currently is going through the crucible of caring for her husband, whose health is in critical condition. She does not deny or ignore these circumstances. Instead, as she has shared with me, her balance and peace come through her faith in Christ. For this woman, faith is the cornerstone of her identity. Faith transcends work, family, and gender role; it provides security, solidity, and peace so that she might live well in the present.

Despite humanity's disobedience, God's redemptive plans will prevail. We still live under the loving mercy of the Sovereign Lord. Over and over in the Scriptures, God calls the people to return, as in Zech 1:2–3. Ultimately, in Christ, humanity is restored and justified before God and joined into the people of God (Eph 2:14–22; Rom 3:20–25).

The great news of the gospel of Jesus Christ breaks down the social barriers that alienate groups from one another: "There is neither Jew nor Greek, there is neither slave nor free, there is no male and female, for you are all one in Christ Jesus" (Gal 3:28). His cross embraces the displaced people of the world. Christ's identification with the poor, lonely, displaced, and outcast opens the possibility for a much fuller inclusion in the body of Christ. Their new allegiance is not to any nation or government or cultural group, but to the God of all cultures. While cultural and ethnic *distinctions* remain, believers always keep in mind their higher citizenship: their shared belonging, together with people who appear "other," to the family of God.[46]

A Distorted Theology of Suffering

Among many Christians, there persists a distorted theology about suffering: the idea that positive thinking, being optimistic, is the only godly way to combat the effects of trauma, suffering, or depression. This approach relies on negating, denying, or ignoring anything that hurts or that requires a difficult process of healing. It also turns that process of healing into a losing battle with guilt and self-blame, as people with psychological or emotional scars try to will themselves into feeling better by thinking positively and inevitably fail to banish the far-reaching effects of their deep pain.

Is this a truly biblical perspective? Believers who attend church services regularly face an added stress, in that they are expected to find a solution to life's problems on their own by listening to sermons and reading the word of God. It is easier said than done. I believe Scripture teaches us to go deeper into the private battles of saints, and that it requires too for the body of believers to be much more in relationship with each other—involved together in the process of sanctification.

When suffering has been prevalent in the lives of believers, these individuals have a desperate need for not only sermons and Scripture, but for shepherd-helpers who can help them over some very difficult places. In order for someone to be able to listen to a sermon and praise God on hearing it, there needs to be a readiness. When it comes to feeding the spirit and knowing the gospel, as Paul says, you must have milk before you can have meat (1 Cor 3:2). This, of course, leads to a true paradox that must be addressed: we are called to rejoice, but we also need to recognize suffering. Any true theology must incorporate both of these aspects, or it will be useless to strengthen the saints and help heal our communities. We are stuck between rejoicing and suffering, like a wheel in motion: between the already and the not yet, between death and the resurrection. In that place of paradox, we will find that it is in relationship with each other that our lives are transformed.

In building helping relationships, we must have wisdom in cultivating trust and the feeling of safety. The importance and difficulty of this task cannot be underestimated. Understanding how God speaks to our suffering

46. Volf, *Exclusion*, 213.

is crucial if we are to obey Christ's command of carrying one another's burdens, and nothing can help us build trust more than pursuing this biblical understanding of suffering and human need. In studying how God responds to suffering, we learn how we should respond. In understanding God's heart for the hurting, we grow in compassion. And displaying that compassion, reflecting it to those around us, leads to trust in relationships that enables true healing to take place.

Bringing together the arcs of both Hebrew and Christian Scriptures, we are overwhelmingly shown that God did not simply throw humanity from Eden. Instead, God seeks out and finds those who are lost, leading them to the place where they will lie down in green pastures. This life prepares us for the life to come, where we will live in a city that becomes a place of true refuge, and where the fruit of salvation blooms eternally. No temple for God and Christ is there; none is needed. As Christ's representatives in this world, we must join God in that rebuilding, seeking out Christ among the marginalized, and bringing refuge to the wounded.

3

When Science and Scripture Unite

THE NEED FOR SHEPHERD-HELPERS once accepted, and the understanding of the city's importance formed, it remains to examine *how* the healing presence of Christ can be brought into the lives of the downtrodden. The Refuge model is one of many approaches to trauma counseling, and I would like to here outline a few other existing models, discussing in the process the unique benefits of trauma counseling that marries faith-based approaches and the wisdom of modern psychology. Often, these two things are portrayed in Christian circles as enemies—secular versus sacred—but I believe this to be a mistake. Modern medicine, science, and psychology can be used together with biblical truth to serve the poor and the marginalized among us, whose lives are haunted by tragedy and trauma.

To set the stage for this discussion, I will use an ethnography report on a real-life story. I will relate this report and the woman's story in full, and then I will use this sample to interact with the various leading experts in the field of mental health, to show how they might approach the difficulties and problems of this individual. For the purposes of this book, I will call this woman Maria, rather than using her real name. Maria's experiences represent those of many marginalized members of the target population extraordinarily well.

Ethnography Report: Maria's Story

Maria's Day at Work

I have known Maria casually for more than fifteen years. She works part-time in a beauty salon owned and operated by a woman from the Dominican Republic (DR). Located in a minority urban ghetto in North Philadelphia, the salon is a friendly gathering place for many Hispanic families. Maria washes hair and cleans the salon. Although she receives government supplementary income (SSI) for a medical disorder, she enjoys working and will take on temporary hourly work whenever the opportunity arises. In addition to her hours in the salon, she sells vegetables and fruits on the streets, and she also sometimes helps another local merchant from the DR.

Her connection to the people from the DR is admirable, especially since Puerto Ricans are not generally embraced by Dominicans because, as with many other Latin Americans, Dominicans resent the political status of Puerto Ricans as US citizens. Many of them look down on Puerto Ricans because they believe that they are given everything by the US government, while other Latin Americans have to make crippling sacrifices to get minimal help from social agencies.

Having known people from many Central and South American countries, I can distinguish accents from Argentina, Columbia, Ecuador, Cuba, and several others. When Maria spoke, I recognized that she had adopted the Dominican accent. During the interview, which was conducted entirely in Spanish (later translated and transcribed into English), I marveled to hear her use Dominican intonations and phrases. Maria is cared for and loved by her Dominican boss and the salon staff through relationships which extend beyond the workplace. Her boss' teenage children have "adopted" her: particularly the middle daughter, who lavishes her with public displays of affection. These relationships have enhanced her social standing in her community and have given her a new sense of family ties and belonging—possibly the source of her Dominican accent and acceptance into DR culture.

I visited the salon one day to observe the atmosphere in which Maria worked and her interactions with the people around her. On this particular day, she was busy with her normal duties: washing hair, sweeping up hair from the floor, wiping counters and mirrors, and mopping the floor. Three hairdressers worked at their stations as several new customers walked into the salon. The owner's husband, Don Juan, came by to drop off some papers, and local people came to greet the ladies or to leave free publications from local newspapers. A number of street vendors from different cultures, including Asians, African Americans, whites, and Latin Americans, came by to solicit customers for their various wares (Spanish music CDs, clothes, bed sheets, food, jewelry). Social greetings came from the old country—men shook hands with the women and with the men; the ladies greeted each other with a kiss on the cheek.

Strangers greeted strangers. People leaving the salon waved to everyone present and said goodbye to the stylists in the same way they had greeted others when they arrived. Sometimes Maria accompanied people to the door as they left.

Since this salon was run and operated by Dominicans (despite its location in a mixed community of first-generation Puerto Ricans and African Americans), its internal culture was reminiscent of the way men, women, and children behaved back in the DR. All seven women stylists—aged from late teens to early forties—dressed in tight, bright clothes, displaying none of the self-consciousness or disgust regarding weight that is so prevalent in American majority culture. Everyone shared lunches and desserts, drinking from the same cups.

The salon filled one large room, big enough to accommodate twenty-five people. The row of stylist's workstations lined up directly in front of five hair dryers. In the back was a small kitchen, where the employees ate, and a bathroom. The owner sat behind the front reception desk, talking on the phone. The CD player on the counter played *merengues*, fast dancing music from the DR. On the opposite side of the room, on a top corner shelf, a Spanish station talk show ran on the television.

Maria worked busily and appeared distant at times. As she washed the hair of a number of multicultural customers, she talked incessantly about her health: bladder pain, MRIs, back problems. She kept mentioning her favorite Puerto Rican physician, who "always took time to talk with me for long periods." Her customers did not protest or change the topic, however. One of her co-workers smiled indulgently and whispered to me, "There goes Maria, talking about doctor's appointments again. If it's not real doctors, then it's dreams she's having."

Maria believes that she receives visions about the future in her dreams—not uncommon in Puerto Rican culture. The practice of *spiritismo*, an ancient religious schema brought to the Caribbean from Africa during slavery, is a part of the culture. Prior to the coming of the Africans, the native Taino and Arawak tribes in Puerto Rico practiced a form of mysticism as well. Dreams and visions played a major part in their myths and rituals, and potions to protect the innocent from the evil spirits were commonly used, especially among the poorer classes of the island. When the Spaniards colonized Puerto Rico, the older religious rituals were assimilated into the Roman Catholic faith. As a Pentecostal Christian, Maria's theology allows for mystical experiences—spiritual and supernatural revelations—through dreams and visions. This is more accepted in her church than in most other Christian sects. To Maria, dreams and their interpretations are an extension of her new faith, sometimes serving as a revelation or warning from God about imminent danger.

This particular salon is located on a long stretch of Fifth Street between Allegheny and Roosevelt Boulevard. The locals call it *La Calle de Oro*, the Street of Gold, or Money Street. It is lined with *botanicas*, occult stores where *Espiritistas* perform magic rituals. These shops sell objects such as statues of saints, rosaries, crosses, oils, incense, herbs, and other paraphernalia for the practice of ceremonies.

Maria seemed disturbed by the loud music, television, and conversations around her. Several people were speaking on cell phones; stylists and customers talked and laughed; the talk show and the *merengue* music blared in the background. She looked at me and said: "*Este ruido me esta matando*"—this loud noise is killing me.

She engaged with both men and women comfortably. She was very attentive to the males, laughing openly especially with an older gentleman who walked in from the street. The doors, both front and back, stood open in the hot sunshine, and I could hear Maria's voice even when she stepped out for some air. Sometimes she talked softly, but other times she nearly shouted. She showed courtesy to all customers and occasionally served as the official translator for her DR co-workers. I overheard her translate a communication between a young African American customer and her boss: quite an accomplishment, since Maria's English ability was limited. The translation involved a request for a particular haircut. Her hands bent, twisted, and turned as she creatively tried to draw an image of the chosen hairstyle. Heads nodded and perplexed eyes moved back and forth, but somehow they all smiled as they managed to communicate. Once she finished her work, she sat down next to me and made small talk. I left the salon in the late afternoon, having scheduled a date several days later for the first interview in her home.

Maria's Home

Maria lived in a small apartment complex designed for senior citizens and disabled people in a low-income neighborhood of Philadelphia. She lived on the fifth floor of an elevator building. Walking down the long hallway lined with doors to other apartments, I noticed the expansive glass windows that made a beautiful display of a church with slender steeples reaching for the sky. Unlike other run-down apartment complexes in this part of town, this one felt safe and secure. As her story unfolded in the days ahead, I could not ignore the contrast between this home and the places her life had taken her. She called the apartment "a blessing from God."

We conducted the first interview during lunchtime. Maria greeted me wearing her hair pulled back and without make-up. She welcomed me with a big smile that gave her mature face a youthful appearance. Her home, impeccably clean and orderly, was fit for the dwelling of the Divine Spirit. Decorated in a traditional Puerto Rican style, the simplicity of her furniture, neatly ordered, made me feel immediately comfortable. Small figurines, pictures, and flower arrangements throughout the house made it a personal place. The apartment was small—a kitchen, a living room, and one bedroom—with everything perfectly arranged.

In preparing for lunch, she had thanked me but declined my offer to bring us sandwiches. On her stove, a pot of boiling Caribbean vegetables made ready for dinner. On the kitchen counter reposed a classic Puerto Rican dish: tomato codfish salad lavished with olive oil. She did not offer me food but asked if I wanted water. In typical Puerto Rican fashion, she gave me a tour of her home, pointing to the different rooms and eagerly showing me pictures of her grandchildren. She pointed specifically to one granddaughter, an eleven-year-old who had been plagued with epilepsy. Maria said that she prayed for the child's health and now she was healed. Maria firmly believed that God healed her granddaughter supernaturally and was grateful that she herself was used as the instrument to bring this comfort. I noticed an open Bible and what appeared to be a devotional book on her sofa. While Maria was Pentecostal, she said that she did not attend services as regularly as she did at first, nor was she praying as she once did. She attributed her bouts with depression as the cause for this change in her devotional life.

A wall unit displayed family pictures of her children and grandchildren, and a picture of an unknown man whom she believed to be her father. Christian music played in the background. Pedro, a little canary and her only living companion, sang for us from his cage by the door as we started the interview.

I could not help reflecting that this was a place of peace after a storm.

Maria's Past

Psychologists, experts in trauma, say that the core of trauma is fear. In the lives of many third-world women, this fear can be traced from childhood through maturing and adulthood: implanted early, motivating a host of poor or damaging choices, and paralyzing the victim's hopes for betterment. Maria's story is no exception.

Maria was born in a small, mountain village in the eastern region of the island of Puerto Rico: an area known for its production of sugarcane and home to the *asucareros*, or sugar-makers. As an agricultural center, it contrasts sharply with its closest neighbors in Ceiba, a refined and comparatively sophisticated group of Puerto Ricans surrounded by a large US military base known as the Roosevelt. The men and women from Maria's village were simple people who lived in isolation from other towns. The town lagged behind others in the region, due in part to the lack of any infrastructure for transportation. Today, the town no longer produces sugarcane, having become an oil refinery center.

This shift from agriculture to petrochemicals motivated Maria's family's migration to the United States. Many families, like hers, lost their communal life in their small country villages. They relocated to Pennsylvania and other farm states, looking for farm jobs, something they knew and felt comfortable doing. Some women of that generation left their families believing it a temporary arrangement, but many never went back, leaving them to live with a silent guilt that affects them to this day.

This village had no electricity, no running water (not even a well to draw water from), no traversable roads (to reach the town one had to travel on horseback), and no plumbing, neither outdoor nor indoor. The houses were bamboo structures with straw roofs. Families cooked outdoors on a *fagon*, three stones with firewood placed on top. Everyone in the family slept in one room, some in the same bed (if they had a bed) or on the floor. After many years, seeing the poverty, the government gave the poor beds: small wire cots that quickly came apart, some with mattresses so thin that they could be folded in half. The mountains live vividly in Maria's memory: "Everything was a mountain and everything went up, up. If you had to get water, you had to climb up, and if it rained, you had to hold yourself . . . and you held on because you didn't want to fall, because there was such an incline." She has never been able to shake off the stigma of her origins in the mountains.

Maria's mountain village redefines what we think of as poverty. Without a source of running water, their water had to be caught in whatever way possible. The people gathered up water from a *poso* or *quebrada* (small ponds or creeks), which might be polluted by human or animal waste. Gathering water was one of Maria's daily chores. The only available fuel was wood, and that too had to be gathered daily from the trees on the mountainside by Maria and the other children. "We were raised in the mountains where everything we needed we had to go outside and fetch," Maria explained. They even gathered food from the mountains, Puerto Rican vegetables like *pana*, *guineo*, or *yame*, some of which might be planted or found growing wild. "Oftentimes," she said, "I would just have to go out to the mountain and get lost in it until I would find these foods and bring them back. I always had to think about where I could go and find these foods. This was every day." Occasionally the mountain would favor the children with a treat of sweet, juicy fruits—oranges, pears, or avocados.

The poor in this mountain village also lacked a dignified way to address personal hygiene. For most, the mountain was their bathroom. Few people had latrines (a cement slab with a hole in the center placed over a pit with bamboo slabs for walls) because there was no place to put them—another challenge from the mountain. Maria feared using the latrine, because the split bamboo walls meant that she always felt someone was watching her. Families bathed in groups in the river where, once again, the lack of privacy engendered fear. If they had no soap, they used leaves.

Maria is one of nine children (five boys and four girls) with the same mother—five siblings had the same father, and the other four were from different fathers. Maria is the fourth child and the oldest of the children with the same father, who "just suddenly disappeared" when she was young. They never saw nor heard from him since. Only the picture of a man who might be her father remains as a memento in her home today. She does not know her precise age, since it may have taken years before her parents registered her birth (due to the lack of money for transportation to the nearest town). She laughingly says her birth date is April 14, 1949 but believes she is, in fact, younger than that.

The Beginning of Sexual Molestation: Memories of Incest

For her first eight years, Maria lived with her grandmother, but when her grandmother died, Maria had no other choice but to live with her mother. Now she wonders if things might have been different had she stayed with her uncle, whose children married well and have good lives. (She wonders this despite the fact that this uncle sexually molested her even before the age of eight, before she left her grandmother's home.)

When Maria returned to her mother's house after her time living with her grandmother, her brothers (who were older) did not regard her as a sister. "I was not raised with them," she said. "I did not have their respect. I look at my brothers as my brothers in my mind only, but not in my heart . . . probably because things happened . . . I would say they desired me." Maria had been sexually active before returning to her mother's house at the age of eight or nine. She sought out boyfriends in her village, and by age fourteen, she had experienced intercourse. Her two brothers also exploited her sexually. "They didn't do any damage to me," she said. "Instead they just used me." She described it as "normal, as if we were a couple. It was the family life that we lived. Maybe they didn't look at me as family." Maria rationalized the experience this way: "Animals too have sexual relationships, and they don't find partners that are perfect. We too are not perfect." She saw herself as the "type of young girl that would attract people." Pictures of her at this time reveal a beautiful Puerto Rican girl, reminiscent of the Maria character from *West Side Story*.

Maria believes that the poverty, the close living quarters, the communal bathing, and the adults who did not watch over their children contributed to a pervasive practice of childhood sexual abuse and incest throughout the mountain village culture. She never spoke to her mother about any of it "because of the shame."

While these sexual practices were prevalent, people yet kept them deeply hidden. Today, Maria speaks of her experiences with deep resignation, relating a story about a father who had children with his daughter: "She forgave him . . . she couldn't do anything else, because her life was already done. She had already done everything, so she can't go back." When Maria sees her brothers now, she doubts her memories: "Is it possible that this could all be a dream? Sometimes I think these are all dreams, because I cannot accept, I cannot look, I cannot see these things." Today, she sees her brothers as lost and feels great compassion for them.

These early domestic attachments and traumas had long-reaching effects for Maria, as is common for all of us. Maria's love and longing for her mother, for example, has characterized her whole life. Her mother was an alcoholic, and Maria and the other children took on the responsibility of taking care of her when she was sick. According to Maria, "Everybody in Puerto Rico was a drinker. Everyday my mother would drink, because I come from a family of people who loved to drink." When the government stipend arrived, her mother would go into town, a day-long journey by horseback and bus. On the way back, she would stop to buy groceries, and the people in the town would get her drunk because they loved to mock her (Maria believes that they loved to mock poor people). Her mother would stumble home, falling-down drunk. Maria was "the one next to her, massaging her body, putting rubbing alcohol on her, and crying for her." She acknowledges missing her mother to this day, but when asked what her mother's ordinary days were like, she finds the memories too painful. "I can't remember; I don't remember a whole lot because I had so many horrible experiences that my mind won't remember. My mind won't give me space to put that in it. To reflect on all these things—I just can't do it. My childhood, how I saw my mother? I just cannot see them in my mind."

Maria has vivid memories, however, of the tropical storms and hurricanes that frequently slammed into the mountainsides of Puerto Rico. To protect themselves, her community had flimsy storm houses (tormenteras) consisting of straw pitched closely over a hole in the ground. They took refuge in the storm houses, waiting minutes, hours, and sometimes days at a time, holding on tightly so that the wind would not sweep them away. The devastation and death were widespread. Now, when Maria hears about storms in Florida, the fear returns—a common phobia among Puerto Ricans of similar background. In the United States, even a mild shower is cause enough for many Puerto Ricans to remain home, missing doctor visits and other important appointments. Because of real and deadly hurricanes in their native land, many suffer from generalized anxiety associated with the weather and travel.

With currency extremely scarce, the mountain village developed its own means of exchange. An egg was valued, as it would purchase a number of things—a pound of coffee, half a pound of sugar, or a large loaf of bread. A laying hen was an important commodity. People would even divide a penny (a centavo) in half to buy small things. Everyone in the town would sell whatever he or she could (tobacco and homemade rum were particularly common sale items).

Poverty took its toll on the social rituals of the culture as well. Not many people married; most people would simply cohabitate. Only the economically better-off would have weddings, riding their horses through the villages to get to the town, which had a chapel. Maria herself remembers few weddings.

While parents baptized their children in the tradition of the Catholic Church, Maria does not remember the ritual beyond it being an occasion for dancing and drinking, as is the case in more affluent cultures. Nevertheless, her community in Puerto Rico did value dancing. Dances were held in people's homes. Maria recalled, "In the evening, we would go to this house. Everybody went. We were there all night, eating and dancing and fighting, because often there were fights over the jealousy of the men, or any small thing." Maria still retains detailed memory of the music. Her family, the family of the father of her children, and members of the community, all played musical instruments and sang. She learned all the songs and all the dance steps. Here, at least, was a distraction that cost nothing.

The people announced deaths (and other significant events) by blowing on a conch or shouting. When a death occurred, the family put the body on view for three days. People loved to come to the wakes, because crackers, cheese, and hot chocolate were served. The body might or might not be buried in a casket. After the burial came the nine days of *resos*, traditional prayers based on Roman Catholic tradition, and accompanied by gifts of food, an incentive for people to attend. The women followed a practice of wearing black to show a time of mourning for close family members, done for as long as the individual chose. In the case of the death of a husband, it signified the woman's promise not to marry again. Most of the people in these remote villages, however, did not follow the rituals of the Catholic Church very closely. Many chapels did not have a priest, few people went to confession, and few attended mass on Sunday. "We had no resources," Maria explained.

Poverty defined the mountain people—both self-perception, and that of greater societal identity. Maria acknowledged that "life in the mountains, and the life of the poor, is one of suffering." She left school when she was in sixth grade. There were times when she did not go to school at all. Even getting to school was a challenge. "We had to cross mountains, rivers, wires, and all kinds of obstacles to get to the school. Many kids were sent but they never went. They would stay in the mountains and in the fields looking for their neighbors, fruits, eating stuff, playing and doing naughty things, but they wouldn't go to school."

Two things kept Maria home: the need to gather water, food, and fuel for the household, and her deep shame over not having shoes. Only one of her brothers completed high school. "The rest of us didn't know how to read or write. We stayed stuck." The mountain people have personal inferiority complexes, according to Maria. When anyone talked about the mountain people on television, her people would cover their faces in shame. Why? "Because we were raised without clothes, or any shoes, or who knows why. You just felt this complex. There was no instruction. That's just the way we were raised."

As a girl from the mountains, Maria behaved shyly, but once she began to mingle with different people, people she regarded as "more prepared," she began to change. She did, however, lead a lonely existence. Seeing her as a hard worker, neighbors would ask for her services. People would say, "Give me that girl so that she can wash and iron for me." The neighbors would come and get her, and she would run to do things for them: washing, ironing, and cooking. "Everyone looked for me. I never had a steady place to live, because really, I was alone."

After leaving school, she went to towns outside her area to work in people's homes. Despite the loneliness, she loved that work enabled her to buy herself things: shoes and clothes in particular. It was important to look nice. She cried a lot because she did not have her own place, missed her mother, and felt isolated. Verbal and physical abuse at the hands of the people she worked for was not uncommon. She recalls feeling explosive anger, feeling "timid and noble, but at the same time strong." She took up smoking and found money "wherever I could . . . I would do my naughty things to buy cigarettes, and I did it hidden." Selling her body was an obvious option for Maria, even then.

Relocating: The Manifestation of Trauma

At the age of seventeen, Maria came to the United States at the behest of her sister. While her siblings wrote asking her to come home to Puerto Rico, Maria has not, in over forty years, even returned for a visit. Eventually all her siblings and her mother came to the United States, settling in Philadelphia. But life for an impoverished mountain girl transplanted into urban poverty did not portend well. The damage had been done: "My memories were damaged, and psychologically I was damaged, especially when it comes to marriage. Today I have a sexual problem. I cannot have a partner because all of this has traumatized me."

Sexual abuse followed Maria across country lines. She lived with her sister in Philadelphia and "had a personal problem with my brother-in-law." Not wanting to deceive her sister, and in order to escape his attempts at seduction, she moved in with "the father of my children," as she refers to him. Maria described it like this:

> In order to get out of that problem, I began to live with my children's father, even if I was not in love with him. I went to live in New York. He took me to the same apartment where he had lived with his former woman: the same bed, everything was the same. His son was in the same bed with us at night, and we had no privacy. This was my life when I got on that Greyhound bus. I realized that was the end for me, and I cried and cried, but I never looked back. I never looked back. I kept going, and I was in the situation for fourteen years.

Family Life: Domestic Abuse

Maria bore her first daughter at age nineteen. The father of her children, a first cousin, soon became jealous and accusatory. "Mistreatment, wounds, physical abuse to the point where I just wanted to die. I would speak to my dead grandmother to take me . . . I would tell God that if I was never going to find happiness, I would just rather die. Because we were raised in the mountains, someone raised like that has fear . . . the fear that you don't know how to confront things." If Maria refused this man sex because his son was in the bed with them, he would beat her up.

In desperation, she turned to counselors and help offered by the Catholic Church. They encouraged her to leave him. Instead, she had an affair. When he learned about it, he followed her to the man's house. He promised her that if she came out of the door, she would find herself in a coffin.

At last, Maria took her children and hid with neighbors. Even when she found a room, hoping he would leave her alone, he would always find her and rape her. His hold over her was strong; despite eventually becoming able to live apart from him, she would go to his house and "serve him as I normally would," leaving only at night. After a failed attempt to live with a friend in another part of the city (once again the issue of jealousy and abuse arose), Maria and her children ended up in a shelter. The shelter helped her find an apartment, but Maria could not rise above her despair. At that stage in her life, she left, abandoning her children: two girls and a boy. She was in her early thirties.

Descending into Suffering: A Cycle of Abuse

Soon, Maria found herself in another abusive relationship with a man—only this one was even worse. "He would hit me, injure me, mistreat me; he would throw hot food at me, destroy my house, my furniture, even my underwear. I struggled so much that I attempted twice to take my life with pills." After a month in a psychiatric ward, he waited for her in the hospital lobby. Only when she promised that she would return to him after moving her family to Philadelphia did he allow her to go.

The next day he went to Philadelphia looking for her again. By this time, her mother had moved, stopped drinking, and had a house of her own. Maria would have moved in with her mother, but she would not allow Maria's abuser into the house. Instead, Maria went with the man, living in the streets, in a deserted house without windows, winding up finally in a shelter. When as an adult her dream of a home with her mother came within her grasp, she chose instead a man she knew would abuse her.

Though such decisions often boggle the minds of those who have never experienced prolonged domestic violence, it is in fact normal—and unspeakably tragic—for victims of abuse to return to their abusers or enter new relationships that repeat the same abusive patterns. A full treatment of these specific effects of domestic abuse on a normal human psyche is outside the scope of this book; for our purposes here, I would merely assert that, far from being weak or foolish (as they are so often judged by broader culture), survivors of abuse and domestic violence are among the strongest and most resilient of us. Maria is just such a one.

Unable to get public assistance because she had family in Philadelphia, she roamed from her mother, to her sister, to her sister-in-law, trying to escape this man's physical abuse. He broke her jaw, permanently disfiguring her, but she did not press charges. His drug addiction influenced her to start using cocaine. Finally, unable to bear it anymore, she fled to her brother's house, where she did not set foot outside for a full year. (If she stepped outside, this man promised to cut her face). Slowly, she began to extricate herself from the relationship (aided by the fact that he went in and out of prison), but her own drug use became more and more of a problem.

Once again, with a new man, Maria sank into a drug-induced depression that left her incapacitated for days at a stretch. Ironically, her old drug-dealer abuser came to her rescue, urging her to get up and asking her to marry him. By then he had contracted AIDS, and she did not feel she could take care of him. Eventually he returned to New York, where he died of a drug overdose. Maria lived in fear for a long time that she had contracted AIDS from him, since she had resumed sexual relations with him. She still fears, despite medical reassurances, that this too will rain down on her as a consequence of her actions. She says she is prepared for that eventuality and knows that she will handle it and not keep it a secret.

When she looks back at her family's history, she recognizes the cyclical pattern within the family: her mother's alcoholism, and the molestation and abuse among her family members. All three of her children are "suffering in their marital relationships with numerous partners." She sees one difference in their patterns, in that her children end the verbal and physical abuse earlier in their relationships. Unlike the social dynamics of abuse in the rural area she came from, with no services available, her children have more opportunities within their reach.

The Years of Drug Abuse

Crack cocaine—in my opinion, the most life-damaging drug on the market—is instantly addictive, cheap, and demonstrably changes the personality of those who use it, destroying parental instincts and rendering people unable to survive without it. As I see it, no other known drug destroys the very essence of users nearly as effectively. I was reminded of this recently when a woman walked into our office, apparently under the influence of crack. She was extremely disoriented and incoherent—almost in a state of twilight, between worlds. Her children had been taken away from her, and she gave me the impression that she had lived on the streets for some time. I knew that she needed some assurance, so in her presence, I called one of our counselors to schedule an appointment for her for the next day. Since she appeared so desperate and full of despair, I showed her great empathy and tried to normalize her struggles as best I could. To my surprise, she allowed me to pray for her. I noticed she did not want to leave our office, but with gentle persuasion, one of our staff walked her out. She never returned to our office. To this day, I have no idea where she is. Calling this drug *evil* is a gross understatement.

Maria's descent into drug addiction continued, and by the time she reached her mid-forties, she was a habitual crack cocaine user. She turned instinctively to prostitution as a way to obtain drugs. She does not remember if she worked as a prostitute for two or three or five years; all sense of time was lost in the blur of drug addiction. By this time, she had become her mother, except with the crack of the inner city rather than alcohol. Like her mother, she went from one abusive man to another. But, unlike her mother, she did not even have a roof (such as it was) over her head.

Maria claims little memory about her time as a street prostitute. "I don't remember these things. God has erased them from me, and he knows why he does that so that I won't have to think so much . . . if he were to leave all that inside me, I would be crazy."

She does, however, remember some things in great detail. "For me, I was already an easy woman," she said. "Now I did it publicly. I didn't care if my family knew about it. I would stand on the corner and wait for a car to pass by. There was no shame. I lost all shame—all dignity." She remembers the detective who paid her a hundred dollars, and the eighteen-year-old "customer" who was a virgin. She remembers being taken away and held captive by three men, eventually talking her way out of a very dangerous situation. Once she yielded to a man's demands at knifepoint. She remembers stealing from K-Mart, desperate to buy crack, getting arrested and landing in jail overnight.

Like her mother, mocked by the villagers for her drunkenness, children who saw Maria on the street would taunt her, crying "Look at the prostitute!" and throwing bottles at her. She says, however, that despite the depths to which she had sunk, "I always knew there was a God next to me." She felt God protecting her. "Something would tell me something was going to go wrong. I sensed that somebody was watching me, and that God would reveal to me that I was in harm's way."

A Long Journey Out of Darkness

The climb out of drug addiction was a difficult one for Maria. She went in and out of drug treatment programs. "I just didn't know what else to do because my heart literally was going to come out of me through my mouth because of the incredible terror that I felt." Her words describe it best:

This panic would lead me to open the Bible and read Scripture. It was there that my tears would flow. In reality, I read but I had no idea what I was reading, but God was definitely using me this way. And then there was a time when I no longer did drugs and I broke the addition to crack through medication. This was in the last hour. Slowly but surely, I started to leave the addiction, until God gave me the strength, and then I stopped.

Maria has been drug-free now for several decades.

She had, however, one last addiction—as she called it—to overcome. Every weekend, Friday, Saturday, and Sunday, she was the first to arrive and the last to leave the dance hall. She danced every dance until she became drenched in perspiration, gasping for breath. The place filled with people drinking, smoking, and fighting. Her mother had died from a heart attack after leaving the dance floor gasping for breath. Years later, she remembered her mother's death. "This woke me up, and I asked myself, 'What are you looking for here?' I could almost hear God saying to me, 'There is nothing for you here, only death and danger.'"

Through a contact at the dance hall, however, Maria finally found her way to the church where she became a "new woman in Christ." Once again, she hooked up with a man, this one fifteen years her junior and a drug addict with epilepsy. He participated in a Christian program in a church close to her house. She hoped to save him from himself and took him in to live with her—only this time, things were different. She gave him three chances to take charge of his health, but he did not do what he had to do. "I was not going to live with a person that has such a weak mind that I have to fight with him because he doesn't want to take his medicine, as if he were a child. This was not for me." This is not to say that she did not have some old lingering doubts from her old way of life: maybe she should have stayed with him—he was sick—"I asked God for forgiveness in case I had done something wrong."

"It's not easy," Maria told me, as we sat at her kitchen table. "It's not easy. It's not easy":

> My testimony is not easy. My testimony is an open book. It is very profound. Everybody has a testimony, but some are more difficult than others. People tell me, "How can you carry all this and still God has given you life?" My psychiatrist says, "You have been a very strong woman. Any other woman like you would have been dead already." But God did not permit me to die. God had something for me so that I could be an open testimony to other people.

He took all those bad things away. I am a new person, a different person. What happened to me in my life is in the past. We are in a fallen world with much sin. All these things happen. Some come out good, others come out bad. Since God gave me the strength to fight for my life through the trials and the battles, he has permitted me to come out victorious.

Making Sense of the Story

Maria's life offers a view into the world and psyche of a third-world woman. These are the people held in Christ's heart: the downtrodden and marginalized of our world. The poverty, lack of education or any kind of skills, incest, alcoholism, domestic violence, drug addiction, and prostitution in Maria's story all point to psychological trauma. If the core of trauma is fear, as we discussed above, certainly this woman's life was all about fear—living in it, running from it, drugging against it, and re-creating it. Her story mirrors that of women I have counseled from the Dominican Republic, Africa, Cuba, Columbia—there are "Marias" everywhere. They come from the third world, and they live in the inner cities of America. She serves as a prototype not so much of the poverty in Puerto Rico (although she is very much a Puerto Rican), but as a trauma victim.

In the third world and the world of impoverished urban America, life means a struggle for survival. The early years of sexual molestations, the constant search for the bare necessities, the labor and the caretaking of others, the abuse and the addiction, all dehumanized Maria. The trauma and violence took ultimate manifestation in the selling of her body. It all points to her deep struggle with a sense of worthlessness as a woman—as a human being. She became a human commodity, used and disposed of at everyone's will.

Tragically, her parents sent this destructive message first and loudest. The abandonment of both parents made for a strong case that she was, in fact, not worth very much. Later, the sexual abuse by uncles, brothers-in-laws, and older brothers further reinforced the lack of worth she felt. She meant nothing to them. Add to this her empty inner life and the lamentable poverty of her country, and the result is insufferable pain.

The trauma of women like Maria cries out for a human response. Any worthwhile ministry or service to victimized people requires a deep sensitivity to the psychological wounds they bear. Their treatment demands careful, but active interventions with these issues in mind. In the midst of the wrenching agony of their lives, they need a compassionate counselor, clinical and practical, who can form an empathic solidarity with their struggles. Only thus can internal defenses be dismantled.

One day, while I walked the streets in North Philadelphia, I saw a living image of the inner world of trauma: a young, crippled Hispanic mother, a crutch under each arm, slowly, painfully pushing her baby across the street in a carriage. That picture expresses these women's experiences—"crossing over," trying to get through life with oppressive and debilitating personal and socio-political structures as obstacles to their progress. We must see them and not turn aside—all of us, ministers, counselors, fellow brothers and sisters in Christ—we must understand the causality behind their behavior, their defeated choices, and their powerlessness. We must understand trauma, and the fear that makes up its core.

Through the message of the gospel of Jesus Christ, the church has the medicine to heal the wounded. Without this medicine of the spirit, many people believe cultural scripts or empty promises: that their pain can be dulled or avoided, even healed, by economic success, drugs, material possessions, sex, alcohol, food, and so on. And when people put their trust in these things to heal and help, the result is more pain, more despair. By the world's unrelenting massive marketing campaign of the flesh, with its false promise of fulfillment, we all wind up—rich or poor—in a state of utter emptiness and meaninglessness.

It is the church's responsibility to guide people to where true healing can be found: in Jesus Christ. We must equip ourselves to help bring about this healing in the lives of the people around us, in our city. And that equipping is not enough unless it involves attention to each person's spiritual state. Even non-believers in the helping disciplines are now open to the irreplaceable role that faith has in the mental health of individuals.

The Social Sciences and Faith-Based Counseling

Within Christian counseling circles, however, people are often asking the opposite question: do secular sciences like psychology even have a place in the healing of human suffering? This question is important to ask, especially for those of us who are trained professionals but who also care deeply about the things of God. Some say the Bible is all we need, and things like psychology and medicine aren't necessary: God already gave us everything in the pages of Scripture. But this idea, though it sounds true in some biblical interpretations, misses the deeper truth: we don't have to choose between the Bible's authority and the usefulness of science. God has given us both.

I am not the first person to say this. The scholar Noel Weeks says that the Bible is not the only book needed in healing work, and at the same time, the Bible *does* speak God's truth to all areas of life. According to Weeks, we Christians are wrong when we think that for the Bible to matter—for it to be reliable and true—it has to act like a science textbook.[1] This is very simple, black-and-white thinking, and even though it seems like a high view of Scripture, it actually takes away from the Bible's importance, because it sets God's Word up for failure. If we demand that the Bible be a science textbook before we'll trust it, that means the second it falls short of that impossible standard, it becomes useless and gets thrown out.

Not only is this thinking too simple, and ultimately bad for our reverence toward Scripture, but it also misses the point. God gave us the Bible to teach us how to live godly, Christian lives, not to train us to be psychologists or nuclear physicists. When we submit to the truth of Scripture, our lives are transformed; and that does not change even when we recognize that the Bible does not contain lists of facts about disease symptoms and modern medicines. As Weeks says, just because the Bible doesn't cover every detail in the world doesn't mean we cannot put our trust in its revealed truth. We can live our lives by the word of God *and* learn from the findings of scientists. This is how Scripture and modern science can work together in harmony as Christ moves among the marginalized.

When we use the truth of Scripture as our lens, then, secular sciences like psychology have much to offer, since the Bible leaves room for the findings of science. Take, for example, psychology as it relates to trauma. I have been astonished and blessed to experience the ways psychology and theology work together to ease human suffering. The work done by Perry on trauma psychology, especially, is breaking ground, particularly in understanding the effects of trauma on the human brain. His research has opened a window into understanding how our brains are designed and what they do, as well as what happens in them when we go through trauma. He studies how brains grow, and in his studies, he has been able to show that when a person undergoes trauma, the brain isn't able to grow normally, in a way that makes that person able to easily live a healthy, productive, happy life with others in their families and communities. Instead, they face many

1. Weeks, *Sufficiency*.

more obstacles than others do, because the "primitive" side of the brain is over-developed, while the frontal lobe—the part that helps us with logic, reason, and wise decision-making—is not well developed at all.[2] Imagine a person who was born without legs into a family of marathon runners. Such a person would be miserable if everyone expected them to win races just like the rest of their family, simply by "trying harder" to make their legs grow. But give that person a racing wheelchair and a trainer, and pretty soon they will be winning races with the best of them.

I offer this metaphor to help explain why even Christians who have undergone trauma find themselves floundering, trying to attain healing solely by listening to sermons or praying. Expecting people's bodies and brains to heal just by going to church, reading the Bible, and praying is like expecting a legless person to compete in races without a wheelchair to speed them on their way and a trainer to help them master it. We as counselors must understand the physical, body-and-brain component involved in healing, as well as the spiritual. This is where we can clearly see how the "secular" and sacred were designed by God to work together in harmony, just as the wheelchair was designed to become a legless person's path to movement and speed, and the trainer's guidance teaches them how to use it. As Perry explains, understanding how brains respond to trauma only makes up part of the picture. Without a trusting environment, without safety, without connection to community, the individual cannot heal. Both scientific and spiritual tools are needed to transform the broken life.

Responding to Trauma: Other Models for Care

Since the mid-1990s, a revolution has been taking place in the field of neural biology, particularly as different advances in science, such as brain scans, have allowed new research in the study of the human brain. Leaders in the mental health field are breaking new ground in their treatment of trauma. Every day, we are learning so much more about the effects that trauma, stress, crisis, and neglect have on human flourishing.

Of course, as I mentioned before, understanding what trauma does to the brain will not heal survivors in itself. It will, however, shed new insight in our understanding of the suffering of many trauma survivors. It also affirms how majestic our God truly is, as we see the genius of creation. As humans, we are more than a body and much more than a brain. Scripture

2. Perry and Szalavitz, *The Boy.*

teaches us that the center of who we are is invisible. The Greek word *nous* captures this concept well, containing the idea of the heart: the central core of being, and the place where our thoughts, will, and emotions reside. It is also a place of great mystery, a center of great redemption and deliverance: a place that belongs to God alone. As we understand more about the brain, we will never aim to replace biblical revelation about *nous*; yet our study gives us very practical insight—insight that will open us to more compassion, understanding, patience, and love.

To see this in action, let us consider Maria's story using the wisdom about brains and trauma that comes to us from the field of mental health. After all, we cannot help to ease the suffering Maria faces unless we can better understand what caused that suffering, and why: an understanding of what happened to her body, mind, and soul, and how that affects her as she tries to form a healthy, happy, godly life for herself. We have established the responsibility that the church has, when faced with stories like Maria's, to help guide sufferers toward healing. We have further discussed the need for spiritual wisdom and scientific knowledge to both be incorporated in this work. Many of the mental health field's existing models for care have a lot to offer in shedding light on these aspects of trauma, and when we work with Christ among the poor, we must aim to use the wisdom of these models *and* the truth of Scripture.

Sandra Bloom and the Sanctuary Model

In her groundbreaking book, *Creating Sanctuary*, Bloom describes her mission as seeking to understand what happens to the body, the mind, the emotions, the social identity, the behavior, and the meaning-making systems of people who are exposed to terror—particularly terror that is unrelenting, repeated, severe, or secret:

> The human organism is designed to function in unity, an integrated and interconnected whole. This is negatively affected by a multitude of stresses—such as biological, psychological, social, or moral—or a combination of these. Regardless of the kind of stress, our capacity for clear thinking is constantly jeopardized by physiologically based, bodily and emotional reactions over which we have little control and about which we often have little awareness.

> Any kind of overwhelming stress produces fragmentation, and like Humpty-Dumpty, the pieces often elude reunion.[3]

In other words, God designed us to be whole—all of our systems working in harmony as we move through life, learning to love and be loved. When trauma invades our life, that wholeness shatters, and our bodies and brains start reacting in strong, often uncontrollable ways, no matter how kind or godly or dutiful we are. In fact, our own strong responses are often a mystery even to ourselves, not to speak of the people around us. This is just how trauma works. It's not the fault of the person who was traumatized. Finding our way back to wholeness does not happen easily, or quickly; it does not happen through sheer effort of willpower or praying; and it certainly does not happen alone.

Early in her book, Bloom reveals her deep optimism as she makes a case for the antidote of trauma. Survivors, she says, have "the capacity for human relatedness to provide the healing integration that is necessary if the victim is to transform suffering into victory."[4]

What she means by this is both simple and profound: the long journey of trauma healing *can* be successful, when we undertake it within the safe and supportive context of loving relationship.

With this belief in the healing power of human relationships, Bloom developed her trailblazing work: the Sanctuary model, initiated as an adult inpatient program at Friends Hospital in Philadelphia. Now, Bloom's model is not shaped with a Christian worldview, and yet with its focus on trauma-informed healing relationships, it harmonizes extraordinarily well with the truth of Scripture. God declared early in Creation that it was "not good for the man to be alone" (Gen 2:18 NIV). If God saw clearly how much we would need each other even in the perfect garden of Eden, how much more do we need one another when we face terror, loss, and violation?

Unfortunately, when dealing with victims of trauma, we have not always understood this truth that God saw and designed from the beginning. In explaining the Sanctuary model, Bloom goes back in time to explain the three main ways humanity has tended to understand trauma and mental illness. This history is a long and complicated one, and a full description of it is outside the scope of this book. In sum, to this day, our society continues to struggle. As Bloom describes, during earlier times, deviance of any kind—people behaving differently from what was viewed as "normal"—was

---

3. Bloom, *Sanctuary*, 15.

4. Bloom, *Sanctuary*, 16.

seen simply as *crime*, with no differentiation made between people who were being violent and people who weren't. No treatment was available whatsoever. Even into the Middle Ages, people tended to view deviance as *sin*, treating the mentally ill as witches, executing or imprisoning them. As society developed, efforts were made to remove deviants from sight, so as to preserve the "natural order" of society. These were the first two ways of understanding: "deviance as crime" and "deviance as sin."[5]

That leaves the third way: "deviance as sickness."[6] Bloom says that modern psychiatry—the era of the social sciences we have been discussing—started when people finally began seeing anything out of the "norm" not as a sign of badness, criminality, or sinfulness, but simply as *illness*. She connects this change to the period of the Enlightenment, when the ideas of reason, liberty, democracy, equality, and human rights became central, which changed nearly every part of human society. In the late seventeenth and through the nineteenth century, says Bloom, all kinds of institutions (like asylums) were founded to deal with and care for those most vulnerable, such as children, criminals, the poor, etc. Though these institutions still often had many problems, they were a sign that we had begun to at least try to help and support people who were struggling, instead of punishing, shaming, exiling, or executing them.

A century later, in 1980, post-traumatic stress disorder (PTSD) was entered into the *Diagnostic and Statistical Manual of Mental Disorders*, and in 1985, the International Society for Traumatic Stress Studies was founded. We were making even more progress in understanding what trauma victims have had to go through to survive, and how truly normal their responses and reactions really are, given what they endured. According to Bloom, "The study of trauma reemerged as a result of the first and second world wars when so many soldiers and POWs returned with what was called 'shell shock' in World War I and 'combat fatigue' or 'combat neurosis' in World War II."[7] Why was this important? Well, by making this diagnosis official, PTSD could finally begin to be understood and studied in a serious way, instead of being shrugged off, ignored, or—as was often done in those days—blamed on the victims (soldiers suffering from PTSD were usually treated as though they weren't "tough" enough). Thankfully, since its first introduction, we have come to understand that soldiers are not the only

5. Bloom, *Sanctuary*, 88.

6. Bloom, *Sanctuary*, 88.

7. Bloom, *Sanctuary*, 17.

ones who suffer from the effects of trauma: that, in fact, far more people than we realize are living with those effects, struggling to make it through and deeply deserving and needing our support.

This is why Sandra Bloom's Sanctuary model has so much to offer us. Though rooted in a secular humanist worldview, its grasp of the hard realities of life for someone like Maria can help guide us as we seek to offer her support on her healing journey. By way of example, let us consider how Bloom might approach Maria if she were a patient.

As a psychiatrist, Bloom's first task would of course be to conduct an initial evaluation. She would most likely diagnose Maria as suffering from PTSD and drug addiction. Knowing that not all trauma results in PTSD, Bloom may also consider major depressive disorder as a possibility, or perhaps a different personality disorder. This is because patients cannot be diagnosed with PTSD unless they do actually have the specific symptoms of this illness. Some people's bodies and minds react to trauma in different ways; not all who have experienced trauma necessarily develop PTSD.

For a PTSD diagnosis, we usually notice three symptoms. First, the sufferer experiences what is called "hyper-arousal," which means they are often in a state of high alert—stress, anxiety, and vigilance even when their surroundings are peaceful. Second, they often relive the trauma—through no choice of their own—through flashbacks, nightmares, triggers, or intrusive thoughts. Third, we usually see the person numbing and withdrawing. Herman considers numbing as a way of almost rewiring the brain: either "a traumatized person may experience intense emotion but without clear memory of the event, or may remember everything in detail but without emotion."[8] In both cases, the brain is trying its best to protect the person from the full force of the trauma. After the traumatic event is over, the person's response can yet seem as strong as though the event were still happening. It is very common for the person's body and brain to still be gripped by these overwhelming responses even decades after the trauma itself has ended; the terror continues to echo through the entire person, body, mind, and soul.

Experts in the field agree that the in-the-moment fight or flight response differs from prolonged terror. Our bodies have this automatic response to danger just as other animals do, either fighting or fleeing when we think we are in danger. Research clearly shows, however, that chronic hyper-arousal is different. A momentary fight or flight reaction usually

8. Herman, *Trauma*, 34.

stays in that moment. Trauma, and the constant intense alertness it causes, lasts and lasts. In this state, the body reacts as though we are in danger all the time, even when we are safe. Imagine a person who caught one quick lungful of smoke from a campfire and coughed a few times to recover. Pretty soon, they would be back to breathing normally. But someone who was forced to live day-in and day-out in a smoke-filled house wouldn't be able to bounce back so quickly. In fact, over time, their very lungs would start to sicken, and eventually, the day would come when they would struggle to breathe even after they managed to get out of that house and into the fresh air at last.

This is often what life is like for people who suffer from PTSD. The repeated experiences of chaos and terror "break" some of their emotions and behaviors, just like the smoke damages the lungs. The numbing and withdrawal we often see in sufferers are like "an internal 'cast' the brain places around 'broken' emotions to protect the break from further harm."[9] Bloom's belief is that, because repeated pain and danger created the problem in the first place—just as day after day of breathing smoke-filled air created the lung damage—only the repeated experience of sanctuary will bring healing. She wants us to work to create loving, predictable, peaceful relationships and communities that will allow those who have suffered trauma to have new, healthy, healing experiences, which can slowly return them to the wholeness that was shattered.

In Maria's case, Bloom would say that Maria's depression, her increased anger and irritation, her states of high alert, and her increased smoking and drinking, are all stress-related symptoms: a few of the many normal ways traumatized bodies and brains try to cope with the abnormal circumstance that is trauma. In treating her, Bloom would likely want to help Maria feel validated. "Of *course* you are struggling in this way," Bloom might say to her. "It makes complete sense. Anyone who had been through what you have would be experiencing these struggles."

When trying to understand why Maria keeps going back to men who abuse her, Bloom would no doubt say this is *learned helplessness* As Bloom reflects, "If we can do nothing to prevent ourselves or someone else from sustaining harm, we experience helplessness."[10] For many of us who have not known abuse, this part of the story especially makes little sense. Why, we wonder, would Maria enter and return to abusive relationships when no

9. Bloom, *Sanctuary*, 34.

10. Bloom, *Sanctuary*, 22.

one likes feeling helpless and being abused? Yet she returns again and again into pain and danger that might seem so avoidable to others.

Bloom would want us to understand that this, too, makes perfect sense when we consider the world Maria comes from. When a child grows up around abuse, violence, and neglect, that child is helpless to stop these things from happening. They learn that the world is a dangerous place, and that they will not be protected. They learn that it is normal for others to hurt them and betray their trust. They certainly never learn to try to leave or change what is happening—how could they? A small child cannot survive in society apart from their caregivers. They are completely at the mercy of the adults in their home, and they have no say or control over whether those adults are safe and kind, or violent and neglectful. All they can learn is helplessness. Nothing else is being taught.

Maria was never taught how to stand up for herself in her childhood. She learned the only role available to her: the role of the victim. She made one decision after another, always from a position of weakness and helplessness rather than strength. Just as the abuse damaged her as a child, so it went on damaging her far into her adult life, because it robbed her of the opportunity to learn how to protect herself and how to leave someone who was hurting her. None of us can do things we are never taught or shown how to do. Maria stands as an example of what happens when a normal person, a person just like the rest of us, is robbed by trauma of many of the things we all need to live a happy, safe life.

One of those things that Bloom focuses on is the ability to do well in school. Early on and into her adulthood, Maria struggled with learning, never mastering the art of reading and writing. Over time, she, like many others, came to see herself as unintelligent. But this, too, was not a sign of anything wrong with *her*. In fact, this is quite normal. "Children who are repeatedly exposed to overwhelming stress," Bloom tells us, "cannot learn as well as more protected children."[11] Yet again, Bloom reminds us here of a truth that is both simple and profound. In order to be able to learn, we need a calm setting in which we are safe and cared for enough to be curious, attentive, and able to focus on new information. How well do you think you would absorb complicated mathematical formulas you had to learn for your job if you hadn't slept in three days and your boss was yelling at you while you tried to concentrate? It's the same for traumatized children. Their small brains and bodies are under threat and danger, and almost all of

11. Bloom, *Sanctuary*, 24.

their energy is going towards surviving; they don't have much to spare for memorizing vocabulary words.

This can go a long way to helping us understand the way Maria kept choosing relationships and situations that re-traumatized her. According to Bloom, Maria's difficulties would not allow her to develop the tools she needed to protect herself from such dangerous situations:

> This phenomenon can interfere with the efforts of others to help the victim. Most helping professionals can give examples of times with someone seeking advice on how to get out of or protect himself or herself from a dangerous situation. Together, the therapist and the victim carefully formulate a strategy for self-protection. In the calm circumstances of such an interchange, the victim is in a state of mind that is conducive to learning. Unfortunately, once the victim returns to the threatening situation, he or she becomes quickly hyper-aroused.[12]

In other words, even when a trauma victim can see clearly once they are out of danger, the moment the danger returns, their brains and bodies get overwhelmed—hijacked, we might say. When these patterns were ingrained early and over a long time, we should not be surprised that it takes a lot of time, patience, and support to break them, and to learn new patterns.

Trauma and recovery require remembering the details of the trauma. In Bloom's research, she quotes Larry Squire, who identifies at least two different kinds of memory, both of which are very affected by extreme trauma. The first is what we consider "normal" memory, rooted in language and reason. It takes a large amount of energy and stems from the part of the brain called the *hippocampus*. The second kind of memory, the kind we often aren't aware of, is emotional and visceral. This kind of memory is stored in our bodies and lives in the part of the brain called the *amygdala*.

Let me give an example. Even when our logical, conscious mind might not remember the time our drunk uncle terrified us by pounding on our bedroom door, our "emotional" memory has not forgotten. This is how we might find ourselves completely confused one day years later when, while reading quietly in our bedroom, our heart rate suddenly spikes and our palms get sweaty when we hear our child banging at the bedroom door because they want us to get them a snack. *Why on earth do I feel so scared right now?* we might wonder. *What's wrong with me?*

---

12. Bloom, *Sanctuary*, 25.

The truth is that there's nothing wrong with us. Our emotional memory is working as it was designed to; it is remembering—even when our conscious memory doesn't—that scary day when someone else was banging on our bedroom door, and there turned out to be danger on the other side.

Under calm conditions, these two memory systems behave normally. But when we are scared or stressed, our amygdala, with its emotional memory, takes over. This is what God designed it to do, to help us respond quickly and without thought to sudden events. (If a tree branch was falling toward your head, you wouldn't want to have to spend several minutes figuring out what to do, right? You'd want to be able to jump out of the way immediately!) But God did not design trauma into our world. God meant for us to live in peace and love, not threat and fear. Because of the fall, the design has been twisted. In a state of high alert, when the emotional memory is triggered, that twisting comes clear; the bodies and brains of trauma victims confuse past events and present realities, making their hearts pound in terror at a harmless request for a snack. They live with an overwhelming sense of fear, even when otherwise safe.

Bloom's Sanctuary model teaches us these facts and works with them when it seeks to help support the healing of those who have endured trauma. It offers great insight into how we can create safe environments that promote well-being and human flourishing for everyone, especially in a counseling setting. We form helping relationships by fostering respect and safety; by encouraging mutuality rather than rough, authoritarian control; and by humbly remembering that change is a process. Healing from trauma, under the Sanctuary model, is all about creating peaceful environments and tapping into the power that safe relationships have to cultivate healing. Above all, it operates out of the Hippocratic oath: *Do no harm.*[13] When we bring a biblical understanding to this model, we simply recognize that all of these truths are according to God's design.

According to Bloom, the brain has a built-in method of living through one event while at the same time tuning into a different reality. This she calls *dissociation*. While staying consciously present on a given task, the brain allows us to unconsciously accomplish another task. A very mild example of dissociation might be a man who daydreams about going for a leisurely walk while he is actually standing in his kitchen washing his dishes. In trauma survivors, dissociation can sometimes take more extreme forms. It is common, for example, to encounter a split personality in the survivor:

13. Bloom, *Sanctuary*, 117.

the adult seeking help on the one hand, and on the other, the unseen inner child who was abused. To Bloom, dissociation is here to help us, especially in high-stress situations. When in danger, we cannot think clearly. When stressed or hyper-aroused, we can quickly get overwhelmed by the strong, sometimes scary feelings and sensations that are happening in our bodies. The fact that we dissociate works as a safety valve for survival:

> By separating thoughts from feelings, feelings from memory, or thoughts from memory, the body protects itself from being overwhelmed. The person is then able to think without being overwhelmed by terror or despair. People can get things back to normal if they have "forgotten" the events, or at least have "forgotten" the disturbing emotions of the events.[14]

As people of faith, we might recognize this as yet another sign of God's original design for our safety and flourishing.

Dissociation does not happen the same way for everyone. Some people faint; others experience selective amnesia, with the brain forgetting specific memories. Still others can remain aware of their lives and what is happening to them, but they detach emotionally, becoming numb. At times, this takes the form of setting aside "our tortured emotions and thoughts and put[ting] the entire conflict into a physical symptom such as blindness or paralysis, a symptom picture known as conversion disorder"[15]—in other words, the emotional becomes physical. When any of these dissociative processes happen over and over, in much the same way as a path in the woods becomes well-worn the more regularly we walk on it, our brains get used to responding this way whenever stress arises. This is especially the case if the dissociation patterns occurred during childhood, or in captivity.

Protecting ourselves through dissociation is a natural response to risky situations, and, as Bloom reminds us, it is a response that makes even more sense in children: "Given the powerlessness and defenselessness of children, dissociation is often the only thing they can do to protect themselves."[16] Like all of us, children are learning to understand themselves and others, and they are learning where everyone fits in the world. For traumatized children, this natural process becomes a nightmare, as they struggle to learn terrible truths and to deal with the ways that trauma interferes with their normal growth and development.

14. Bloom, *Sanctuary*, 33.

15. Bloom, *Sanctuary*, 33.

16. Bloom, *Sanctuary*, 77.

Children raised in abusive, violent, neglectful homes have never learned how to think "in a careful, quiet, and deliberate way. They have not learned how to have mutual, compassionate, and satisfying relationships. They have not learned how to listen carefully to the messages of their body and their senses."[17] How could they? Their caregivers' dangerous behavior made such learning impossible. This places a child at a great disadvantage in forming and sustaining strong and healthy relationships.

Bloom's research on trauma, with its strong scientific foundation, gives us insight into what happens inside the brain and the rest of the body when we are exposed to traumatic events. She looks at the way in which our brains affect how our bodies feel, and vice versa. She insists that we take a holistic view of the person who is suffering. Because of this, her treatment plan is able to take into consideration many inner, hidden realities that cannot be seen when first meeting and interacting with a person. This points to the seriousness of trauma and helps us to understand that trauma affects who we are at every level—body, mind, and soul. For us as believers, we would recognize this as pointing to the sacred image of God placed within each of us—and perhaps we can better appreciate why God devotes so much time in Scripture to commanding that we love one another as ourselves.

Bloom also stresses how important it is that trauma counseling work in harmony with other disciplines, such as psychiatry, medicine, sociology, psychology, anthropology, and theology, to name a few. She recognizes that we do not need to choose just one or two sources of wisdom; we are free and even encouraged to draw from many such sources. Such interconnectedness helps us see how complex human suffering and affliction truly are, and in so doing, we are protected from trying to deal with a complex problem with nothing but simple solutions. Her model's openness to this interconnectivity makes it an excellent partner to the wisdom of Scripture in bringing Christ's healing to the wounded.

Bloom does a great service to those who suffer when she recognizes that being traumatized is a disease, not a crime or a sin; yet at the same time, she does not limit the hidden strengths and resources in human life. She points us to recovery by explaining how trauma affects the brain, the body, and the way in which we see the world. In order for us as caretakers to be of any help to the traumatized, we must understand this area of human experience. Bloom's illumination of these realities makes us much more sensitive to the complexity of trauma.

17. Bloom, *Sanctuary*, 37.

Given this complexity, we should remember that experts are still to this day doing research into trauma and its effects. We do not know everything, and we must not act as though we do, as though we have no more to learn and are correct about everything we currently know. The field of neuroscience is new and quickly evolving, and findings that emerge over the coming years will no doubt teach us much more than we know now—and set us straight about some of the things we think we know. That is the gift of science; like Scripture, it teaches us humility, and an openness to learning and growth, for only God has perfect knowledge. Though not religious, Bloom understands this need for wisdom from many sources. To Bloom, mental health care is not self-sufficient. It will need to cooperate with and draw on multiple fields and social systems to deliver the best healing that it can to each hurting individual.

We must also take care to avoid perpetuating victimization by over-emphasizing the power of the brain, making it seem as though victims are utterly helpless. Here, too, we see the wisdom in marrying scientific research with scriptural teaching. We can hold these truths in tension: that while yes, we are vulnerable to trauma and its damaging effects on our brains and bodies, at the same time, we as human beings are responsible for our actions. By God's grace, we have a part to play in our own healing. Our choices and our efforts *do* make a difference.

Healing from trauma needs to promote safety on all levels: physical, psychological, emotional, and spiritual. The Sanctuary model gives us a good example of common grace, and it offers so much good to those who have suffered immensely. As Bloom's model displays, most helpers—faith-driven or not—enter the field not as laboratory types, but as lovers of people. While the scientific theories, the training, and the theoretical frameworks help us produce models that can aid in alleviating trauma, the most powerful tool for trauma healing is a caring heart infused with the gospel. This goodness in relationship brings healing where the most perfect knowledge of brain chemistry would prove sterile and powerless.

Bruce Perry's Model

Another source of wisdom with regard to trauma and childhood is the work of psychiatrist Bruce Perry. According to Perry, it is crucially important that we understand how big of an impact trauma has on us, especially when it takes place early on in life. Perry believes that these damaging experiences act like templates for the rest of our lives. His research focuses on trauma in children, seeking answers to several key questions: 1) what makes a child more inattentive than others their age; 2) what happens in a rapidly developing brain, when a child is sexually abused as a toddler; 3) how does the stress of poverty affect children; 4) why do some children have speech and language delays; and 5) does stress during early life have an impact on the development of the brain? Early influences, he says, can leave imprints on the brain that last a lifetime.

Perry also discovered that the connection between parent and child is crucial to brain development. Our brains were designed to perform thousands of complex tasks, managing and overseeing all of our emotions, thoughts, and behavior. Early childhood trauma gets in the way of this, preventing the brain from working smoothly. Sometimes, Perry explains, the brain is so badly prevented from developing normally that a victimized child can actually have entire regions of the brain that either developed too poorly, or that are not under the person's control. Perry believes this can be important to know when working with someone who survived trauma.

The human brain develops in stages. The most primitive, central areas, starting with the brain stem, develop first. As a child grows, each part of the brain after that—moving out from the center towards the cortex, the outermost layer—undergoes important changes. But in order to develop properly, each area needs certain things to happen at the right time, regularly and predictably, for the right amount of time. We can use the metaphor of baking bread to understand this. Anyone who has made bread from scratch knows that, in order to end up with a normal, healthy loaf of bread, you need to start by combining the right ingredients; then you need to knead the bread over and over for a long enough period of time to allow the dough to form; and then you must give it time to rise, repeating this pattern once or twice until the bread is finally ready for the oven. If these steps are done out of order—if we try to bake raw, unmixed ingredients in the oven, for example—all we would end up with would be a messy kitchen and no bread to show for it. Our brains are similar. In order to develop normally, all the steps need to be present, and in the right order.

In a healthy childhood, the major part of the brain that is forming during the loving care of an infant is the part that learns that other people can meet our needs: "If I cry, someone comes and makes me feel better." Perry calls this a "rewards system," which acts to relieve stress. A baby whose thirst is quenched, hunger satisfied, and anxiety calmed by a caregiver, experiences pleasure and comfort and learns that these lovely feelings come from *other people*. As Perry says, "This interconnection, the association of pleasure with human interaction, is the important neurobiological glue that bonds and creates healthy relationships."[18] In other words, the belief—developed through repeated experience—that "other people make good things happen to me" is a very basic and important belief our brains need to have if we are going to want (and be able) to connect with others and bond well with them.

When loving care establishes this belief during the "sensitive period," or the child's first three years of life, the brain develops normally. However, children who "receive inconsistent, frequently disrupted, abusive or neglected care" may never be able to form this belief in the same easy, early way.[19] After all, their tiny brains were not learning that other people make good things happen. They were learning the opposite: other people bring pain, and terror, and abandonment.

This is especially clear in Perry's work with emotional development after abuse. The mirror neuron—a part of our brain that helps us imitate what someone else is doing, such as a baby smiling when its mother or father smiles—plays a crucial role in forming good relationships. Empathy originates here, as parent and child imitate and reinforce each other with both sets of mirror neurons reflecting each other's joy and sense of connectedness. In contrast, Perry explains, if a baby's smiles are ignored—if she's left repeatedly to cry alone, if she's not fed, experiences no tenderness, is rarely held, or experiences abuse—the positive associations between human contact and safety, predictability and pleasure, may not develop:

> The price of love is the agony of loss, from infancy onward. The attachment between a baby and his first primary caregivers is not trivial: the love a baby feels for his caregivers is every bit as profound as the deepest romantic connections. Indeed, it is the template memory of this primary attachment that will allow the baby to have healthy intimate relationships as an adult.[20]

This has great implications for trauma treatment later in life. We know, as Perry says, that "the brain needs patterned, repetitive stimuli to develop properly. Spastic, unpredictable relief from fear, loneliness, discomfort and

18. Perry and Szalavitz, *The Boy*, 85.
19. Perry and Szalavitz, *The Boy*, 85.
20. Perry and Szalavitz, *The Boy*, 91.

hunger keeps a baby's stress system on high alert."[21] As in our bread meta-phor, our dough will not form properly, or rise when it needs to, if the steps of the recipe do not happen in the right order (or at all). He explains that receiving no consistent loving response to fears and needs prevents a child from developing the belief that human contact is a good thing.

If children are neglected, they learn that the only person they can rely on is themselves. But the good news is, we *can* unlearn some things and learn new ones—especially when we are still children. Once we understand how our brains need regular, positive experiences of security and love, such experiences can be offered in the counseling setting and relationship. Perry's approach to treating children, therefore, first examines which parts of their brains didn't get the chance to grow well, and then works to provide the missing "ingredients" to help the brain grow in a healthy way.

According to Perry, "Numerous animal studies showed that even seemingly minor stress during infancy could have permanent impact on the architecture and the chemistry of the brain, and therefore on behavior."[22] He would begin here with Maria. In understanding her, Perry would be in-terested in tracing Maria's moral development. In his work with trauma, he concludes that genetic tendencies and environmental influences can shape our decisions, which in turn affect our later choices and ultimately form our character. He does not believe in the "abuse excuse" for violent or hurtful behavior (that being abused means it's okay if we inflict abuse on others), but he has found that the ways trauma shapes and damages us can certainly make it much harder for us to make good choices and envision different ways of behaving other than the bad ones we were shown. In looking at trauma through the lens of brain chemistry and moral development, Perry would observe pain and fear in Maria, but also great courage and humanity.

Perry's main belief is that to understand trauma, we need to under-stand memory. To appreciate how children heal, we need to understand how they learn to love, how they cope with challenges, and how stress af-fects them. By recognizing the destructive impact that violence and threat can have on our ability to love and work, we can better understand how to nurture the people in our lives, especially the traumatized children who later become adults.

In Perry's treatment plan for Maria, he would most likely try to provide the safe, loving experiences she did not have when she should have, during

21. Perry and Szalavitz, *The Boy*, 113.
22. Perry and Szalavitz, *The Boy*, 1.

childhood. Since she is an adult, he would have to alter his approach, doing much more "teaching" than he likely would if he had been treating her as a child. Any treatment would take place repeatedly and consistently.

Perry never uses punishment, force, or pressure in treatment, as he believes these make the suffering worse. Instead, he would use music, dancing, and massage to help soothe the lower, more "primitive" parts of the brain—like the terrified amygdala we discussed earlier—which were launched into disorder and fear so early on and never received the calm, loving environment needed to grow healthily. Perry would try to explain to Maria a concept he terms "splintered development": in trauma, a child may reach a certain biological age, but inside she is functionally younger. This is normal for traumatized children; a child who, on the outside, is ten years old, might act in ways we normally only see a three-year-old act. Chaotic and neglectful families contribute to this problem.

Perry also uses "induction techniques"[23] that help with breathing, enabling Maria to handle things better when she feels overwhelmed. As he puts it, "The key to recovery, then, is to get the patient to understand that her perceptions aren't necessarily reality, that the world might not be as dark as it seems."[24]

Clearly, what happens during our childhood years will influence the adults we become. Looking into these areas may help someone like Maria understand herself and develop some new habits, thoughts, and practices that will help her recover. This new interest in understanding the brain, especially in the field of trauma, is a strength in Perry's work. His guiding beliefs and values are sound: the focus on parental love and support for healthy development; his refusal to let early trauma excuse perpetuation of abuse; and his stressing of consistent, calm, loving environments without resorting to harsh measures during therapy. His work is crucial to mental health care and trauma counseling, and just as with Sandra Bloom's Sanctuary model, Perry's model has a great deal to offer in working with victims of trauma.

Perry helps us open our eyes to new wisdom in the field of mental health. Not only does he illuminate how trauma affects the brain, but he also brings us to a position of truth within psychology. In his quest to learn why some abused people grow up healthy and responsible while others respond to abuse by inflicting it on others, Perry takes an important moral

23. Perry and Szalavitz, *The Boy*, 197.
24. Perry and Szalavitz, *The Boy*, 195.

stance: that, as quoted above, humans need to learn to become humane. In today's field of mental health, many people avoid language that sounds moral or ethical in tone. But Perry's words bespeak a strong moral code, and a much-needed one at that.

Perry's written work gives us much insight into children and trauma. His life commitment to this work led him to found The Child Trauma Academy, an interdisciplinary group of professionals focusing on high-risk children and their families and how to best improve their lives. Not only does Perry want to provide the best possible care for people suffering with various mental health problems, but he also wants to teach others how to do so. And in his focus on the individual's moral responsibility, we see a prime opportunity for a cooperative relationship between science and Scripture, for only through the agency granted by bearing responsibility for our actions—in spite of undergoing trauma—can survivors heal in a full and lasting way.

Maria in the Church

As we have seen, secular trauma counseling models have much to offer, but they do not operate with the fullest picture possible. Without being able to walk alongside the victim in *spiritual* healing, they cannot bring *complete* healing. For that, the "Marias" of the world often turn to the church—and what do they find?

They find the other side of the coin: a faith community that has much to offer, but that is not operating with the fullest picture possible, either, because of its inability to walk alongside the victim in *complete* healing, not solely *spiritual* healing. The time has long since arrived for science and faith to work together in the service of the downtrodden. There exists an alarming gap between the church and the sufferer, and as frequently noted by church leaders, the secular world always seems to be several steps ahead of us in responding to the challenges of our times. Many sufferers seek help from their fellow believers with the hope of finding solutions to their troubles and are sorely disappointed—or even re-traumatized.

Oftentimes, too, the hurting and the broken walk away from church empty and burdened with guilt. Why is this? With the church as a hospital for the hurting and broken, can healing come to American society? Surely, given our increased understanding that faith must play a major role in bringing healing to individuals, the church is best suited to supplying this lack. Yet even amongst believers, we often find the same lack, the same need for healing, as we find in the rest of secular society. The need for the people of God to attain emotional wholeness—via both secular and sacred avenues—cannot be underestimated. If the church can become strong, vibrant, and healed, it is my belief that the outcome will be a shift: not only inside the walls of the church, but in society as a whole, where the evidence of the Spirit will triumph over the flesh.

A Recovery Model

Can we then establish an alliance between science and faith: ministries in which the church and the sufferer can join hands and seek healing together? Not only is the answer *yes*, but already this movement is underway, and has been underway for some time. The ministries in which I served can stand as a model for other communities of faith to follow as we seek to join in the work of Christ among the poor. For more than two decades now, pastors and lay leaders have partnered with each other in the city of Philadelphia, to challenge conventional wisdom and understand mental illness from within a Christian faith tradition that has enriched its efforts with science. Many of our lenses for viewing the world and each other changed in this work, but I think one of the most important was our understanding of what "healing" or "recovery" truly mean. In the past, we saw healing as something total and final—a complete absence of any symptoms and a new, pain-free life. But as we experienced Christ's healing in the realms of trauma and mental health, we came to understand that healing and recovery can be better defined as a *process of change* through which those burdened by suffering begin to see themselves with more compassion, to live a self-directed life, and to rebuild meaningful and fulfilling relationships in the heart of their community.

The pastors and lay leaders in the church who had undertaken the job of bringing this vision to pass were taking up a heavy burden. Many of them were overwhelmed and weary and had prayed for a professional, faith-based counseling outreach that not only dealt with the daily hardships of people in the urban setting, but that also took the next step in providing trauma-informed and culturally relevant service to those within their churches. And that is precisely where the Place of Refuge came in.

The Place of Refuge: Merging Faith and Science

By God's sovereign grace, the mission and the vision of the Place of Refuge sought to answer these things—to provide God's people with the tools and skills necessary to help bring about true healing in the lives of people in the city. The center began by offering professional counseling services; by giving training in counseling techniques and skills; and by working together with pastors and lay leaders in their care for the people of God who were struggling with various counseling needs.

In this realm of counseling that marries the spiritual and the scientific, Dr. Langberg stands as a prime example. In her book *Counseling Survivors of Sexual Abuse*, she provides a biblical, theological foundation for counseling work that expresses deep care for patients and attends to their treatment in a holistic way. Her principles played a large role in forming the Refuge model, as she offered initial encouragement and mentorship in the development of a model of care for the urban poor. Her work truly sets the high standard for Christian therapists to follow, providing a Christ-like understanding for clients.[25]

My own time as founder, director, and as a counselor at the Place of Refuge has long seemed to me a perfect symbol of the way Christ's work among the poor happens from the ground up: a dynamic, organic kind of growth which has its roots not only in formal education or experience, but in the power of God to choose a movement's leaders, its influencers behind the scenes, and all the many contributions and strengths needed to give a healing ministry its shape. My tenure there, from 2004–2015, marked a time of seeing God's wisdom and mysterious way of bringing the right people together at the right time for the work that is needed. As one mentor of mine put it, "How many Puerto Rican women are called to this unique community in North Philadelphia with previous executive corporate training, excellent clinical supervision and mentoring, a theological doctorate from a reputable seminary who knows this community well, has lived in it and walked its streets for decades now, and has come from the same culture, sharing the language, values, and worldview of the people being served? How many have been mentored and supported by the local Hispanic clergy, making this start-up possible because of the trust and credibility of her life and calling?" This perfect match of work to those best fitted for it can be seen everywhere in God's kingdom, from the seemingly small

---

25. Langberg, *Counseling Survivors.*

to the seemingly great. Instead of false humility or self-effacement, we look around us in wonder at the way God equips us and others for the tasks at hand, and we rejoice to see this in ourselves as well as in those around us. Recently a dear friend gave me the image of a constellation of stars all shining side-by-side as a way of envisioning this aspect of the kingdom of God; and as we all shine to God's glory, we remember Paul's words: "What do you have that you did not receive?" (1 Cor 4:7).

Though my time in the leadership there has ended, this collective "shining," and the fruitful marriage of science and faith, continue at the Place of Refuge to this day, and in other ministries like it in Philadelphia and elsewhere. Secular and sacred work toward a common goal on many levels in this center; on the administrative and credentialing level, the center is scrutinized and undergoes regular audits from the city's credentialing agency. Refuge's "best practices" must pass audits wherein administrators, counselors, supervisors, and clients are interviewed separately and then feedback is given, along with a formal report. (This is known as an "NIAC" audit.) These regulations protect and serve the community, the counselors, and the center itself, allowing eligibility for funding and granting Refuge credibility as a community mental health specialty clinic.

On the level of counseling, too, sacred and secular unite to serve the community. The Refuge model incorporates the neuroscience of trauma into its in-house training for staff on all occasions, at every level: during training and ongoing supervision, both formal and informal. Every moment is a teaching moment, every challenge an opportunity to pull from science's wisdom to achieve a greater understanding of how our brains and bodies work—all informing trauma intervention, treatment planning, and measurement of progress. This approach spills into the therapy sessions with the people the center serves, as well. By using simple charts and easy explanations of the different components of the brain and the way in which trauma may have taken shape in someone's life, counselors can plant the seed in the person that there is much more going on internally, and that their struggles are normal, understandable, and—most importantly—changeable.

This model employs *informed compassion*: a humane method in which counselors share scientific facts within the framework of the larger battle. This equips the patients with the knowledge, skills, and techniques that give them an opportunity to overcome—taking steps into the fray—motivating them to move forward while looking at the reality of their suffering. Counselors do not deny, oversimplify, or overstate a patient's suffering; rather, details are presented at their pace, with their consent, and in a fair, objective way.

This takes place in a three-fold manner: first, by creating the sacred ground of the clinic. Each life must be treated with respect and dignity. From the moment the person steps into a reception area, those serving them must practice true reception; they must be embraced—not physically, but through the peaceful nature of the environment. Shepherd-helpers must always respect the integrity of personal space, for those they are helping, and for themselves. Therapists must also learn boundaries to distinguish their role and responsibility to the client, holding confidentiality in high regard, yet remaining informal enough so people can sense the humanity and authenticity of the professional who is providing them with care.

Second, care teams must be rich in both faith and cultural sensitivity. At the Place of Refuge, staff create a cultural framework that is familiar and comfortable to the large number of Hispanics they serve. For instance, in the case of Puerto Rican culture, strong emphasis is placed on family structures beyond that of the nuclear family, with members cultivating a warm atmosphere of celebration and open arms, all of which increases quality of life. In honoring these cultural values, the center tries to recreate them within the culture of the Place of Refuge. The learning curve for professional therapists can sometimes pose quite a challenge; many graduate programs do not teach their students about cultural awareness. Having the right leaders to develop and shape a ministry model can also be difficult, as most leaders in the field of mental health never had to incorporate cultural factors as well as faith.

Thirdly and lastly, those offering care must strive to create a spiritual refuge. In the center, prayer to Jesus Christ is foundational. Since the Place of Refuge is a faith-based, trauma-informed center, they naturally use Christian practices that are meaningful to the individual who seeks their help.

The outcome is redemptive and powerful to behold. And this outcome is measurable in a few ways, the most significant of which is how often patients come for sessions. The United States national average for mental health visits is one; most patients do not return after the first visit. At the Place of Refuge, if a patient comes for at least one visit, he or she will return on average for *twelve* visits.

Even more astonishing than this, however, the center's patients show incredible progress in their symptoms. By the time most patients leave, those with trauma no longer have the symptoms of PTSD dominating their lives—especially if they continue with counseling for at least three years in a row. Over the two decades I spent walking alongside survivors of trauma, I saw it happen again and again. Major symptoms connected to people's diagnoses began to dissipate in the face of loving, trauma-informed, faith-based counseling.

The Refuge Model and Maria's Story

What, then, might we expect to see if a woman like Maria were to come seeking care from a faith-based, trauma-informed counseling center like the Place of Refuge, or any other modeled along these lines?

To answer this, let us first consider her story. In many ways, Maria represents a typical Puerto Rican woman. From early childhood, superficial things (attractiveness, desirability) determined her worth and power in the world, and the way she was constantly treated as a result of these things led to a lifestyle of suffering and being sinned against. Like most *Puertoriqueñas*, Maria worked at an early age in order to care for her physical appearance. It ruled how others saw her and how she saw herself.

While her dreams and aspirations were not different from most Puerto Rican women, she had far too many tragedies and abuses visited upon her that shattered her dreams. She followed the cultural script for her gender, placing all her worth and effort into beauty, submission, and service to family, but without a strong foundation in her family of origin—without protection and acceptance from her parents, and respect from the males in her life: brothers, uncles, and cousins—this cultural script betrayed her. Instead of a rich female life, she lived an increasing succession of traumatic events.

In a healing counseling relationship—when the patient's trauma has been chronic and prolonged—something called "reenactment" makes the recovery process all the more complicated. "Reenactment" takes place when the person expects the same kinds of wounds others inflicted on them to keep happening. They are on the lookout for those wounds, bracing against them, and often reacting as though the wounds are indeed happening again (or about to happen) even in situations where they aren't—where the person is perfectly safe. The survivor cannot be blamed for this, because they have never experienced safety and righteousness in close relationships; instead, they expect bad treatment or evil intent, making change difficult:

> The protracted involvement with the perpetrator has altered the patient's relational style, so that she not only fears repeated

victimization, but also seems unable to protect herself from it, or even appears to invite it. The dynamics of dominance and submission are reenacted in all subsequent relationships, including the therapy.[26]

Here we must take care. Clearly, God desires for us to stand whole, not to live trapped in learned helplessness or other old, self-destructive patterns. Our role as shepherd-helpers and companions in such cases is first to discern where the person is inside, then to prayerfully ask the Holy Spirit to guide us in relating to someone suffering this way. How can we help break the cycle of helplessness? If that cycle remains, consequences are painful, not only to the survivor, but to all others in relationship with them. It can break fellowship with believers and hinder communion, leaving no place for safety or trust. When learned helplessness holds sway, the relationship is so fragile that the smallest slight can tear it apart. Considering the depth of the relationship between spouses, or parent and child, or sibling and sibling, or neighbor and neighbor—nothing can cause greater alienation and isolation than this. Nothing could be further from God's heart of reconciliation and healing.

In Maria's case, this learned helplessness left her in a state of isolation until she became friends with her Dominican boss. At that point, the cycle broke. Her boss embraced her as one of her own family. By simply loving Maria and understanding her, and by trusting her with the responsibility of washing hair in her beauty salon, Maria's boss planted the seeds of the first healthy relationship of her life.

Secular trauma counseling models like Perry's or Bloom's have many strengths; and yet, for the Marias of the world who long for spiritual as well as mental and physical healing, these models are like rich ground waiting for the spring planting that will bring a harvest. When earth and seed unite—when science and faith join hands and work in tandem—God moves within the human heart to bring about lasting transformation. Christ directly changed Maria's life, through the care and guidance of another person, a shepherd-helper. She no longer lives to satisfy men's sexual demands, vainly hoping to be cared for. Instead, she has conquered her additions; restored her family ties; found a community in which to be accepted and work productively; established the home that eluded her for so long; joined a church that supports her faith; and is growing in her service and love of others and her acceptance of herself.

26. Herman, *Trauma*, 138.

This is why the Refuge model—which I will outline in more detail in the next chapters—weaves spirituality and prayer into its counseling framework. The Marias of the world need scientifically informed care, and they need to experience sanctuary; but they also need the message of Christ and the hope that God gives.

The church cannot stand silent here. We must reach out and help. We cannot and must not continue to turn away from the thousands and thousands of traumatized women and men living in the third world—the one that exists abroad, and the one that exists at our doorstep, in our inner cities and elsewhere. The Christian church has failed so many victims by ignoring the reality of their suffering. Christ would not have done this, and we must not, either. By loving them in a transforming way, one at a time, we can lead them to a new life in Christ. The dark side of Maria's life has been retold too many times. Let us help bring about the transforming side of Maria's life in the lives of other hurting people.

4

Shaping the Refuge Model

TRANSFORMATION, IN THE KINGDOM of God, has a way of spreading outward, of blessing the suffering individual and then rippling outward to bless in turn everyone touched by that person's life. This is true of trauma survivors and the downtrodden, and it is true, too, of those of us who put our hands to the plowshare together with Christ and seek to become a healing presence in a struggling and wounded world.

In the remaining chapters of this book, I share the story of how Refuge's efforts began to ripple outward, influencing the community, and bringing transformation and growth to other congregations and organizations. I then provide in full the training modules we developed for lay counselors and that we used and refined with time and experience. My prayer is that readers who are eager to join in the work of Christ among the marginalized will here receive encouragement to do so—not merely in a general sense, but through the specific example of our efforts in the city of Philadelphia—and that the training material will serve as a launching pad for initiatives within your own congregations and ministries.

May our eyes, newly opened to the realities of trauma, and our hands, willing and extended toward those in need, be offered up in service to our God of goodness, who multiplies our efforts like loaves and fishes to feed the multitudes.

The Refuge Story

Since the founding of the Place of Refuge, we were called upon many times to speak to and train staff throughout the Philadelphia area relating to the center's work: trauma treatment, cross-cultural competency, advocacy, lay counseling, and faith-based intervention. Over the years, we spoke to nearly two thousand people in non-profit organizations, churches, schools, governmental organizations, and university-based centers. Public awareness of our work came through word of mouth; we never marketed. This awareness only increased with time. In 2012, we spoke to over six hundred people in six organizations, and in 2013, we spoke to almost nine hundred people in fifteen organizations.

Many of these secular and Christian organizations came to the Refuge staff because they recognized that the center was filling a particular need not being met elsewhere. No one else in the state of Pennsylvania had established a city- and state-credentialed, faith-based counseling center that so specifically addressed the issue at hand: the impact of trauma on the lives of low-income minority populations (largely women) in an inner-city setting. We served an area recognized as one of Philadelphia's most needy—a low-income neighborhood widely known for crime and drug addiction.

Those interested who came to see our facility recognized that the center had a successful model, operating under less than ideal circumstances and on a low budget. Because we served a largely Hispanic neighborhood, we provided services with a strong emphasis on understanding the unique cultural needs of our clients. Our faith-based orientation had special appeal to local Christian communities. To the Christian congregation listening to Christ's mandate to serve the poor and minister to the least among us, the Place of Refuge stood out not only as a therapeutic model, but as a cross-cultural model and a Christ-based model. As we went out to speak to different church groups, people in the congregations expressed the desire to help, articulating a calling to a ministry they believed they could fill. In most instances, we heard this from lay people, not professionally trained psychotherapists or licensed counselors. These lay audiences were increasingly telling us that they wanted to get involved, that they wanted to help others—to walk beside the sufferer.

It is important to note that we recognized anyone impacted by trauma in its many forms and manifestations must be treated in a particular way, and such people must, in the long term, get treatment from trained professionals; in no way could or should a lay counselor act as a substitute for needed professional intervention. We also recognized, however, that trained lay counselors could play a key role in supporting the traumatized individual and those who suffer in various ways, bringing them to a place where healing can begin.

All too often, the person most in need of professional intervention is the least inclined to seek help. (The high incidence and rising rates of suicide sadly attest to this.) Particularly within a church's close interactive ties, a lay person sensitive to the signs of suffering and trauma can help bridge that gap. The person suffering from serious psychological issues often does not want to acknowledge their state, but they may express concerns more freely to a lay person than to a mental health professional. Gradually, over a number of years, we learned what people wanted to know and what they needed to ask. We listened to them and, based on our professional experience, built presentations and workshops around those expressed learning needs. Many presentations were of short duration: an hour to an hour and a half in length.

Some organizations asked for one-day workshops. Before long, we had developed a large volume of training materials on a wide variety of topics related to the learning needs of lay counselors.

As we spoke to more and more groups, it became clear that there was a role for trained lay counselors. With the proper selection and training of lay personnel linked to an infrastructure to support a program, we could help establish a ministry to the suffering within an organization. Churches provided an ideal place to pilot such a program.

Three trainings in particular stand as examples of the evolution of the lay counseling model we eventually developed, and I examine each in turn, giving a look at each teaching experience as a case study, in order to offer some idea of what such training entails and how it can fit logistically within a given organization.

These experiences, and the wealth of information and materials gleaned over the years, led to the development of the training modules I have included in the next chapter. These topics encompass the basic body of knowledge needed in order to train a lay counselor to function within a designated organization. They are intended to represent the basis upon which lay counselors can build their knowledge, skills, and expertise in identifying and guiding the individual in need of counseling services.

We recognized the potential for significant outreach through the training of lay counselors, who so often function as the entry point to counseling when traumatized or hurting people reach out to them. Our experience spread out to other community organizations and churches as a model to intervene where the greatest need exists, and it provided us with the foundation in the form of training materials for establishing a viable, effective lay counseling program.

Developing the Modules

Encountering the Need

In 1992, I was introduced to the Summer Medical Institute (SMI) by Dr. Klaus, founder of Esperanza Health Center, and my boss at the time. The Institute is a health outreach program and takes place over several weeks in the summer, combining the efforts of volunteer medical students and local church members to go out into the community and provide free healthcare services and the love of Christ.

Back in the 90s, however, it started to answer a very specific community need: measles. During those early years, public awareness had risen dramatically for HIV and AIDS, and funding for research and treatment had begun to flow even into our community. These issues needed attention, but unfortunately, so did many other grave health concerns that were receiving no such funding and support. While the money came pouring in for HIV/AIDS patients, in the little streets of Philadelphia, *The Philadelphia Inquirer* and *The Post* began reporting widespread child deaths from a lack of immunization. Before talk about health reform was politicized, the Hispanic pastors and their constituents, along with a few medical doctors at Esperanza Health Center, made a commitment to do something to stop these children from dying. SMI became an evangelization model, wherein medical students were matched with local families and churches. Small portable medical stations were set on strategic corners, where volunteers administered free immunizations to children all over North Philadelphia.

As a visionary, Dr. Klaus understood the significance and impact that indigenous, lay leadership would have on the mobilization of Hispanic congregations in North Philadelphia. The community was in much distress—everywhere, one saw signs of human misery, hopelessness, and despair. We saw this in all social institutions except one: the Hispanic church, alive, radiating with the love of Christ, and ready for action. What better way to answer the community's need than by forming an alliance with pastors, lay leaders, and medical students?

This is what SMI did. It helped to form a strong bond of Christian love among Christian medical students, local church leaders, and a hurting community, thereby confronting a serious problem. A look, therefore, at the historic beginnings of SMI work gives a deeper understanding of the development of the Refuge model and helps to inform the work we undertake today, each in our own communities.

Responding to the Need

Dr. Klaus shared a special love for those most marginalized and impoverished, as did the pastors and lay leaders. Under her guidance, SMI took care of providing the immunizations and getting all the medical equipment and injections necessary. My friend Michelle (a Westminster Theological alumnus) and I coordinated the outreach program for its second year, after a gifted team of staff members from Esperanza Health Center had piloted the program the previous year. Together, we developed a curriculum and presented it to the late Reverend Fred Estrada, outlining the entire outreach, which included cultural competency, a mini socio-economic bio-assessment, and selection and screening of participating churches and coordinators.

Reverend Estrada led the way, as he was highly respected and esteemed by the Hispanic clergy in North Philadelphia. A Hispanic Christian family embraced each medical student; the families and their churches would host the students during the entire summer outreach. This was a cross-cultural experience that all involved would never forget: Hispanics hosting and leading, and medical students (mostly Caucasian) being introduced to, and serving, the least among them—children. But we did much more. We brought the message of the gospel, prayer, and hope, and we connected the people to the faces of Christians in North Philadelphia.

We worked with over thirty medical students that summer from all over the United States, and with ten leading pastors and their congregations. This was quite a commitment! The outreach was so successful that to this day, SMI continues vibrantly through the efforts of my former colleague and friend, Dr. Laura Layer, and sponsored by Tenth Presbyterian Church.[1]

1. For more information on the Summer Medical Institute's current program, visit their website at www.mcophilly.org.

This emergency, and the church's response, laid the groundwork for the ongoing work that unfolded over the next decades. SMI had made that initial connection between local branches of the church and Christian healthcare workers. The pastors, through the strength of trusting and safe relationships established by SMI, were ready to tackle other health challenges in the community head-on. And soon it became clear that trauma demanded our attention, along with other silent killers in our community, i.e., depression and anxiety. Pastors especially knew that despair and hopelessness were killing the joy in our families.

And so, once again, Reverend Estrada and Dr. Klaus formed another great plan to introduce or pioneer a lay counseling outreach program to the same churches, pastors, and volunteers. They hired me full time after SMI to lead in this outreach and act as a counselor. I still remember all of the community pastors and their lay leaders[2] who participated in that first meeting. We formed a circle and began in prayer.

Unfortunately, the program did not get off the ground at that time; a philosophical difference between Dr. Klaus and I hindered the development of such an outreach. I adhered (fanatically, I now think) to the existing Christian lay counseling models as I knew them at the time. This meant no integration between their theological prepositional approach and forming a biblical model for counseling treatment by incorporating secular theoretical models. Dr. Klaus, being a medical physician, strongly adhered to the use of integration, in particular the medical model. Her argument was that the existing Christian counseling models were too narrow and therefore not appropriate for the urban Hispanic population we serve. In retrospect, she was right. (Ironically, I have come to share her view quite strongly, as chapter 3 of this book attests!)

At the time, however, I was young and (quite frankly) too caught up with my own act. Since we could not agree, to my shame, nothing ever fully developed the way SMI had. I have no doubt we could have gained the full support of the pastors, but the differences between Dr. Klaus and myself were too deeply felt. Yet the Lord knows all things, and truly God's timing is always the best. Over the past two decades, my relationships with

---

2. The group consisted of Reverend Fred Estrada; Reverend Danny Cortes of Nueva Esperanza; Reverend Bonnie Camarda, Living Word Church; Reverend Efraim Cotto, Iglesia Bautista; Reverend Fidel Echevaria, Iglesia Evangelica Bautista; Reverend Sergio Martinez, Iglesia Sion; Reverend Luis Centeno, Bethel Temple; Reverend Raul LeDuc, Iglesia Zion; Hermana Pina, Iglesia Cristiana Misionera; Reverend Raul Palomino, Iglesia Ebenezer; and Dr. Manuel Ortiz, Spirit and Truth Fellowship.

the Hispanic clergy and lay leaders have been mutually respectful, as we have maintained a sincere affection and an eternal bond. After the initial SMI outreach program, connection continued with the local churches in such a way that, in its time, the Place of Refuge had a strong foundation from which to minister. The pastors kept seeking direction from us for various counseling needs in their congregations, and this formed the basis for a strong relationship in which I acted as a consultant to the churches in handling different counseling challenges. Ultimately, these congregations would make referrals to our ministry at the Place of Refuge. But in the meantime, a few opportunities soon arose to do some preliminary lay counseling training—and thus the seeds of the Refuge model for trauma and lay counseling were sown.

Community Voices in Developing the Refuge Model

How Interns Helped Form the Training Curriculum

Ministry endeavors are never a "one-man show"—or at least, they ought not to be. The work of Christ is bigger than any one individual, and the strongest movements in God's kingdom are those that are helped and shaped by many voices, not just those of figureheads or leaders. The Refuge model was just such a community effort, and it was shaped by all those who encountered it, as well as by its early envisioners.

One group whose voices played a large role in shaping the model was interns. In the early 2000s, we began to have a number of graduate interns at Refuge from various schools, including Westminster Theological Seminary, Biblical Theological Seminary, Palmer Seminary, Arcadia University, Temple University, and Eastern University, to name a few. A rare event, but highly beneficial to our young ministry, was the opportunity to provide a site for a psychiatrist resident to complete a one-year field experience with us. She counseled an individual for that year using prolonged exposure therapy, a powerful trauma-informed method, typically used with war veterans who suffer from PTSD.

As much as Refuge contributed to the education of their interns, then, their presence and feedback contributed an equal amount to the development of the training model. Very early on in our decision to partner with different educational institutions, and to offer internships, it became clear that the circumstances in our urban population presented us with the opportunity to expand our understanding of how best to help our people. Even before we officially became a certified non-profit organization, during supervisory meetings, Dr. Langberg[3] and I discussed how to contextualize the existing theoretical models to meet the needs of our focused ministry group: Hispanics and African Americans. This challenge increased later in our growth when we began to accept one-year internships at our new facility in North Philadelphia. We knew we would need to provide additional training to strengthen our interns during each one-year practical experience with us, and ultimately this need helped shape the eight training modules we developed. Their training needs perhaps most informed the development of our module on suicide assessment and precautions, as will be elucidated later.

All of Refuge's interns had to attend in-house training required by the credentialing agency. The Place of Refuge also required training in the eight modules of our counseling model, which overlapped and added to the credentialing agency's basic requirements. According to one intern, Trish:

> The value of the training and education that I am receiving as an intern at the Place of Refuge is difficult to put into words. I am currently in my final semester of graduate school, and while I am receiving an excellent education in school, my internship and the training I have received at the Place of Refuge is filling in some important gaps: helping me to connect what I am learning in school and actually meeting the needs of each of my clients . . . Understanding how a theory works is very different than putting it into practice in a culturally and biblically appropriate way, which is what the Place of Refuge is training me to do.[4]

From New Counselors to Seasoned Therapists

Interns and staff alike at the Place of Refuge found the training process essential to enriching their practice. As we incorporated their feedback into development, we found that both groups of professionals—the experienced and the new counselors—brought unique perspectives to the process. The

---

3. Dr. Langberg served as my mentor throughout all of these years, and for over two decades has given professional guidance and support to thousands of individuals and families through mentoring me, without taking a dime. From her initial role establishing Refuge to this day, she continues to be a loving presence in this calling.

4. Email message to author, February 5, 2014.

new counselors entered the counseling room equipped with what they needed to help clients; even seasoned therapists found that the training informed and significantly improved their effectiveness. One of them, Sharon, explains it in this way:

> As we developed the lay counseling training, Refuge staff participated in trainings on the different subjects included. This participation benefited both new and seasoned counselors. New counselors were learning the model for the first time; they were also interacting with clients and the information for the first time. This helped develop educational materials that prepared new counselors for difficult situations, such as suicidal ideation and anger management.
>
> Seasoned counselors were able to speak to these subjects, but they did not have as much experience with new findings on trauma and the brain, or other physiological aspects of trauma. In this way, the training added to their expertise and experience. It also seemed the training helped both seasoned and new counselors in the area of teaching self-care. I have found through experience and conversations with others that, whether you have been counseling for two years or twenty, we are always learning. At no point in counseling others do you say, "I know all there is to know." That is a dangerous place to arrive. Researchers are breaking new ground in understanding trauma and the brain; cultures are growing and changing. Our world experiences new types of trauma through natural disasters and war. We have to be open to learning and understanding so we can help those around us. In this spirit, the lay counseling training developed by Refuge continues to evolve and educate.[5]

Preliminary Church Teachings

As with the interns and staff, we found that early training experiences with local churches also served to shape and improve the final modules. The first teaching we did took place over several months in the late 90s, led entirely in Spanish at a leading Spanish-speaking church in the area. The church approached us for help in responding to a crisis involving the sexual abuse of children by a trusted and close family friend. The crisis intervention included identifying victims, helping them get professional counseling, helping adults make calls to ChildLine to report the abuse, finding resources for

5. Email message to author, February 10, 2014.

additional services, speaking to the general congregation about the abuse and ways to maintain support, and addressing the Sunday School children using the video, "Strong Kids, Safe Kids," featuring the Fonz.[6] We collaborated with other social agencies that advocate for children, and we were present in court cases involving the perpetrator and sentencing. Finally, in the years following the crisis, we also provided literature and an understanding of trauma and its implications to the individual, family, and congregation.

During the second training we held, a few years later, we used Dave Powlison's CCEF material, "How People Change."[7] This training again took place over several months, this time at Bethel Temple Church, pastored by the Reverend Luis Centeno. The lay counseling contingent, both male and female members of the church, were all first- and second-generation Puerto Ricans, born and raised in North Philadelphia. We used videos, held discussions, and did role-playing exercises. Gathering data and understanding the process of lay counseling was key in the training. Unfortunately, despite the training (which even reviewed a sample of a policy for sexual abuse), the group never quite became integrated and established in the church, partly because of a change of pastors and my own lack of long-term vision. This led us to further develop the training component today that helps organizations put a structure into place internally that will ensure the strong continuation of lay counseling efforts, long after the training has concluded.

Finally, a few years after the Bethel Temple training, we undertook another Spanish-led training session for the Philadelphia congregation Iglesia Sion, held in the home of the deacon and deaconess. This was for a Pentecostal group of middle-aged women, a few men, and the church's pastor. Topics included listening skills, mental health diagnoses (depression, anxiety), family problems, dealing with parenting, and conflict resolution. We also had a medical doctor from Esperanza speak on the physiological causes of illness. The group's traditionally Hispanic overtones, the strong Christian bond, and the mix of cultures in the trainers (Caucasian and African American) made for a unique, enriching, and lovely experience.

These initial lay counseling training efforts bear only slight resemblance to the more polished program we eventually developed. In those early years, my focus was splintered between developing the Place of

---

6. Hauser, *Strong Kids.*

7. This curricula material can be found on the organization's website: www.ccef.org/curriculum/how-people-change-curriculum.

Refuge, undertaking a degree from Westminster Theological Seminary, and struggling with multiple sclerosis (MS). For the young Place of Refuge, the credentialing application and the process at both the state and city levels was a prolonged journey. Attending seminary also required much energy and concentration. Ultimately, however, despite the illness and the academic challenges I faced, I have experienced personally that nothing is as true as the love of Christ and the promise that when we are weak, we are strong in him.

In the following years, we led several more thorough lay counseling training seminars, each of which will be examined in more detail as case studies shortly. By that time, the Refuge model material was in a far more finished state, and the feedback from these experiences helped put the final touches on the program. Yet without exception, each church training experience contributed to the model's development, and encouraged and strengthened us in our work. As Refuge staff member Sharon summarizes,

> I was blessed to participate in some of the early trainings in the development of the lay counseling program . . . It was clear from the beginning that the people participating wanted to learn. They were not there just to vent or talk about their experiences. They wanted to grow as lay counselors and learn how to better counsel people in their church. This was evident through the number of questions they would ask. From day one, when they saw the outline for the trainings, they asked, "Can we have more time?" Each time we would give a training session, they would have more questions and ask if we could continue to talk about the subjects.
>
> They enjoyed the practice and shared how they planned to use the information given . . . Each time the training was given, people would seem hungry for more information. You could see they had a passion and heart for serving others. They had a love for those who have been wounded from trauma. They also were unsure where to start or how to help these people they felt called to walk alongside. Through the lay counseling training, they started to feel as if they had a tool belt to wear. Not only did the counseling provide resources, but it also provided encouragement and love to the participants.
>
> God's presence was always clear in each training experience. With a difficult subject, it was important to fill it with God's joy. There was never a shortage of this joy with each training experience.[8]

8. Email message to the author, February 10, 2014.

Church Case Studies

In this section, we will explore the experience of three case studies from Refuge's teaching, reflecting on the outcomes of each. These experiences may be used in shaping further training groups of these kinds, or in determining the feasibility of forming such a group within your own organization. Speaking and training opportunities were made possible for us in many different venues over the years—university lectures, delivering papers at conferences, giving a presentation to specialized groups of various types—and these opportunities did bear fruit. Ultimately, however, the best format for our lay counseling training is the model outlined below. For churches to successfully establish outreach efforts in the community, the training should take place over several months. Only a substantial investment of time can form a strong lay counseling outreach that will have longevity and lasting effect.

Case Study 1: Tenth Presbyterian Church

As with all of our work, these studies began with a need. I have heard the need expressed in many different ways from many different pastors. In this first instance I will share, it started with a phone call, followed up with a meeting, and finished with a letter. The special projects coordinator contacted me to convey the church leadership's hopes for the training in their congregation. "Our motivation," she wrote,

> is to relieve some of the pressure on our elders by equipping a few individuals in each parish with training to better allow them to come alongside brothers and sisters who are encountering personal difficulties and to help them apply biblical theology and principles to their relationships and day-to-day life. This would better allow us to provide intermediate care for those who need a little more input than their small groups might provide, but who do not really need professional counseling.[9]

The participants in this group were hand-chosen by the church elders: eighteen people, three from each parish, people whom the elders had confidence in as a part of the team. Elders had complete leeway in their selection, and in some cases, the elders themselves enrolled.

9. Email message to the author, January 6, 2012.

From our meeting with the deacons, we identified possible topics most relevant to the known needs of the people in the congregation. Along with this, we discussed potential presenters and their specialties coming out of the Place of Refuge.

The training lasted for a period of twelve weeks, with two-hour meetings following the Sunday morning church service. This guaranteed a high attendance rate and also set the tone. Many of these stretched into extended question and answer time at first, but I saw the group develop a nice camaraderie and a kinship, and our scheduled two-hour sessions became longer through the participants' enthusiasm for the material. As they came to know one another in this church training, many confessed it felt unlike anything they had experienced before in their church lives. For the first time, they had begun experiencing a deep sense of community with each other. During this twelve-week period, members showed consistency in attendance, in their participation, and in their excitement and connection with the material.

Behind the scenes, our staff formed a very cohesive, loving, and caring team as well, evident in the gathering of training materials, the organization of slides and presentations, the assembling of supplemental materials and handouts, and in providing transportation and equipment setup. While some of the other presentations we conducted are not represented here, other staff and our psychiatric resident gave presentations and trainings as well. During the initial weeks of the training, the group asked that we consider a new module: one that indicated their commitment to initiate counseling outreach. We saw this as a sign of their ownership of the project, which was critical to the success of the training and its relevance to this congregation.

The modules below do not correspond directly to the final modules of the Refuge model, which will be outlined in full in the next chapter. We conducted this training program with this church as a pilot course, using the experience to refine and expand our teaching model. Therefore, the modules we followed in the pilot course naturally shifted in later years to incorporate further identified areas of need in training.

The First Module

The first module was significant in setting the course for the entire training. The participants needed to understand the framework, role, responsibilities, and the limitations they must undertake in any kind of counseling interaction. We made the boundaries of their counseling relationship a priority for the training, holding an extensive discussion on the topic as a follow-up. We gave special attention to distinguishing between lay counseling and the professional therapeutic relationship: a crucial item for the overall protection of the church.

The Second Module

Following that module, we focused our attention on what we called "The dos and don'ts," or those things to cultivate or avoid in a counseling relationship. This module presented basic guidelines and emphasized the importance of causing no harm to the person seeking help. We followed this with training on building a relationship with the sufferer, and included teaching listening skills, so that the trust and safety of the lay counseling relationship could be established.

The Third Module

We then hosted a module on trauma. In churches, as well as in the population at large, this topic garners great interest, particularly in understanding how to give care to the traumatized. We explained that Christians are not exempt from having a traumatic history, and only recently have some churchgoers felt able to share their stories more openly, without feeling shame or guilt over not being able to "free themselves" from trauma's effects. They yearn for their brothers and sisters in Christ to understand, accept, and love them, but many are mis- or uninformed when dealing with trauma—a real tragedy, not only for the survivor, but for the entire congregation, the church, and for society.

The Fourth Module

We proceeded to cover the topic of suicide prevention and intervention. The church, as a builder of individual lives and communities, often finds itself confronting individuals who experience true ambivalence about living. Because of the extreme seriousness of suicide threats, it is imperative that any lay counselors understand what protocol to follow in such a situation.

The Fifth Module

Cultural competency training matters greatly as we walk alongside those from different backgrounds. Traditionally within the church, mission organizations have understood the role that culture and language play in sharing the gospel of Jesus Christ with peoples of different nations. In the urban context, the role and significance that culture has in the lives of people is unavoidable: globalization and immigration have brought more people, languages, and ethnicities together in close proximity than ever before. Cultural competency, therefore, must now extend beyond mission organizations to include the whole of the church, and this is especially true of someone desiring to be a lay counselor.

The Sixth Module

In an urban setting, the violence found in the inner city makes loss and bereavement a reality for so many individuals and families. That reality demanded a module addressing this issue. We aimed to provide participants with an understanding of this form of suffering, giving them the skills to reach out with compassion and mercy to those who are hurting and broken.

The Seventh Module

As the group requested, our final module consisted of common-sense practices that would accomplish an effective outreach effort within the congregation to those who suffer. In addition, staff from the Place of Refuge gave presentations on a variety of topics, including Parenting and Family Counseling, Trauma in Children, and the Psychodynamic Therapy model.

Outcome of the Training

After concluding the training, the associate pastor and the training participants met for lunch and a debriefing in order to determine where next to take the project. The group agreed to select a coordinator who would bring the effort together, and then arrange for them all to meet once a month. They requested that I act as a consultant as needed. I met with the administrative coordinator one additional time, learning that the participants had been utilizing some of their acquired skills in lay counseling relationships with members of the congregation. As the cohort began to be formally established, the trainees were actively using the skills gained from these lessons, and the deacons and deaconesses confided in me their belief that the training enhanced their ministry. They also established a prayer ministry involving active listening.

Our training with this church had a direct impact on our work in a number of excellent ways. The church contributed financially to the Place of Refuge on an annual basis, and many individual members did as well. At one point, during a financial crisis, the church gave the center an additional grant to sustain our operation. Further opportunities for teaching, community education, and presentations arose from this connection, such as presenting at the day-long urban ministry conference "Walking Like Jesus" in spring 2013 and participating in the church's global outreach day in the fall of 2013.

Case Study 2: Christian Legal Clinics of Philadelphia

Christian Legal Clinics of Philadelphia (CLCP)'s mission is "Doing justice with the love of God by advocating for those in need in Philadelphia." They invited us to give a talk entitled "Christian Advocacy in the Counseling Context" on March 23, 2013, which thirty of their lawyers attended.

The core of the training focused on advocacy within a counseling relationship. This relationship dictates that the counselor play the following role: first, to validate the person's journey (as contrasted with condemnation, criticism, and judgment); second, to build a trusting and safe relationship (as contrasted with abuse, betrayal, slander, and violation); third, to establish true equality and personhood—inclusion and embrace, leading to solidarity (as contrasted with exclusion and inequality). Finally, the counselor practices advocacy as experienced in *shalom*, the peace of God, as contrasted with alienation from God, self, others, and the environment.

We asked three questions regarding advocacy: *Where did we come from? Where are we now? and, Where do we want to be?* We set these questions within a North Philadelphian social context to include the educational attainment of the given population, poverty and wealth levels, and crime and community dynamics, along with the health status of the average person.

Our counseling model considered the strength of the individual: resources, social network, and interdisciplinary collaboration, all of which have special relevance for the legal community. The CLCP's efforts in North Philadelphia fit into the framework of advocacy called for in this model particularly as they aimed to influence public policy and resource allocation. They also played a role in health advocacy, as it focuses on improving access for the disadvantaged.

The presentation moved on to the context of inclusion and economic disparity, since the CLCP played an important role in supporting and promoting healthcare rights and policy initiatives. We also discussed three specific mental health agency requirements: first, the utilization of evidence-based counseling models with a pay-for-performance reimbursement structure; second, service from professionals in faith-based counseling; and third, the offering of contextualized, culturally competent services. Finally, we demonstrated the growing demand for specialty counseling in trauma.[10]

Outcome of the Training

This session demonstrated the value of networking and community outreach in forwarding Refuge's work. One of the participating lawyers became interested in the ministry and later interviewed to become a board member at the Place of Refuge. Through this training session, we established a referral relationship with the CLCP. Refuge staff members served on a number of occasions as consultants to CLCP lawyers who needed to debrief a counseling situation or needed referral services for a client.

Case Study 3: Biblical Theological Seminary

In May of 2013, the director of the counseling department at Biblical Theological Seminary in Hatboro, PA invited us to present "Cultural Competency and Trauma within Hispanic Cultures" at their Global Trauma Recovery Institute (GTRI). I gave this two-hour presentation to over twenty students, all of whom had taken related online courses and were connected somehow to trauma work. Some were master's level counseling students taking the course as an elective. Students came from many different countries, such as Africa, Romania, Jordan, Haiti, and diverse communities in the United States.

---

10. Trauma-related disorders ranked highest among our target population, with mood disorder at 39 percent, adjustment disorder at 28 percent, and post-traumatic stress disorder at 16 percent (based on an internal report at the Place of Refuge).

In response to my opening question, "What would you like to see in your hands at the end of our time together?" students gave such a multitude of answers that I course-corrected. Rather than continue with a prepared text, I spent the time answering their many questions about our experience at the Place of Refuge. The questions focused mostly on how treatment intersects with faith, though they also wanted to know about the facets of culture, mental health problems, and the urban population.

In summary, I reminded students of the need for basic assessments of trauma, looking at biological causes and explanations first, then assessing emotional and psychological causes, and then, finally, doing a spiritual assessment. We also discussed the role of collaboration with pastors, the place for prayer and the Holy Spirit in counseling, and the strong bond of Christian fellowship between counselor and client when they seek guidance from God together.

Outcome of the Training

As a result of this training, we contracted with Biblical Theological Seminary to allow graduate students to complete a one-year internship at the Place of Refuge, with the agency providing clinical supervision and oversight of their required counseling practical curriculum, building an excellent Christian counseling outreach in the urban context.

These highly qualified graduate students made a significant contribution to both the field of counseling and the kingdom of God, and the financial remuneration involved alleviated some of the strains on a young startup organization such as Refuge. Additionally, the students brought with their youth a great idealism and a profound, transformative faith. They represented the bright hope for the next group of Christians who administer the truth and mercy of our Redeemer to the hurting and the broken in our midst.

Feedback: What We Learned

As we went out to other mental health agencies and as community organizations reached out to the Place of Refuge, the depth of people's hunger to hear and learn amazed us, and their incredible compassion for the suffering they saw around them moved us. They saw the impact of trauma in individual lives, in families, and in the community at large. The state of learning readiness within the community was clearly there, and the literature today supports the concept of a holistic approach. The mental health community believes in it; they now desire the practical, how-to steps to make it real. At each presentation, we saw participants come alive at the prospect of implementing the approach we had tested and championed at Refuge. We felt that we had taken some solid steps in the trail-blazing path outlined in the literature and codified into the city's credentialing regulations.

In the midst of these teaching experiences, we learned an important lesson about working within the existing structure of a church or agency. Participants in the training programs left filled with eagerness and ready to go to work, but when the organization had no structure in place, no designated leader to take hold of that enthusiasm and turn it into action, the flame died quickly. Within any organization, faith-based or secular, work such as this must have the support and endorsement of those at the top; without it, nothing will happen. In a church, the pastor, by definition of role, has the designation to lead the congregation in the proper direction.

A surprising and rewarding lesson was the positive impact that our training and outreach efforts had on the staff at the Place of Refuge. As invitations grew and more and more speaking opportunities presented themselves, the center's staff rallied to the occasion, pulling together the volumes of training materials, handouts, PowerPoints, workbooks and the like needed to make each professional presentation. Our large manual of training materials was not my work alone. It was in the truest sense a joint effort, representing the heart and soul of every one of Refuge's staff members.

Preparing for training opportunities did not occur as one more task in an already over-extended workday. It became a learning opportunity for everyone, myself included; and as such, we all found ourselves tapping into unsuspected creativity, learning and contributing to something bigger than ourselves. The potential community contribution these speaking engagements represented, and the opportunity of spreading the word, were not lost on anyone. Before undertaking this journey, we believed that we had a good team; in actuality, we discovered that we had an excellent one.

Intern and Staff Feedback

The input of our staff and interns contributed in an irreplaceable way to the growth of the ministry over the years. Examining the words and perspectives of these individuals gives a sense of the sort of work that is involved in ministries of this nature, and the fruit borne in the community as a result. Our professional therapists also had important reflections to share regarding the work of the Place of Refuge, and specifically the relevance of this work to the cultural problems we face in the United States, ministering to an impoverished minority group in an urban setting. Consider the following report from a Refuge intern:

> One thing I have been learning during supervision at Refuge is how important cultural competency is, especially in relation to trauma. Understanding culture and where a person is coming from is an integral part to the therapeutic relationship. Cultural understanding should be the basis [of] all therapeutic decisions, because culture shapes a person . . . [One client] I worked with was a survivor of much trauma and abuse. Ms. Hernandez helped me understand her background and how a survivor of such significant trauma views the world. She gave me useful analogies that would be helpful to this woman in light of her culture and context. She continually reminds me that remembering this woman's culture, her background, and her story are important in how I relate to her in session. Ms. Hernandez helps me as an Anglo-American to understand the different cultures I work with. The training I am receiving at Place of Refuge, specifically in regards to cultural competency and trauma work, fits in to what I am learning in my classes. Ms. Hernandez continually teaches me practical ways that culture comes into play during sessions, and I am learning how trauma is different for each person because of their diverse backgrounds.[11]

As one of our staff corroborated, "All good counseling centers should encourage their therapists to stay aware of the ways culture and race influence the therapeutic relationship." Her comments expanded upon this thought:

> Ethically, therapists should constantly be monitoring their own biases and cultivating appropriate professional supports in order to minimize any negative effects these biases may have on the therapeutic process. The model at the Place of Refuge not only . . . expects this basic level of ethical practice, but also goes a step further . . . [encouraging] therapists to not only consider personal issues, perspectives, and biases, but to also become increasingly mindful of larger social, cultural, and racial issues, and the impact of those issues on our clients. In this framework, it is essential for therapists to understand broad concepts such as institutional

---

11. Marianne, email message to the author, February 10, 2014.

racism and white privilege, and to always keep these larger societal dynamics in mind throughout treatment . . . .

If I were to summarize the model at the Place of Refuge in relation to cultural and trauma issues, I would say that we as therapists work intentionally at empathy and understanding. We are *not* looking down on "those poor people in North Philadelphia" or writing off the neighborhood as a lost cause. Instead, we are walking alongside. We promote dignity. We are putting ourselves in a position to understand, to feel some of the pain, to sit with injustice, and to invite Jesus into all of it. Our clients are brave. They have persevered under excruciating circumstances. They have survived and learned to thrive even in the face of unthinkable horrors. We are called by God and passionate about bringing the hope of Christ as we sit alongside and help to carry heavy loads of pain.[12]

Others reflected on the significance of how the Refuge model incorporates secular and scientific findings into clinical practice, gleaning the best from modern psychology and other fields of study that can shed light into the plights of each client who needs help. Rather than developing a model that avoids such resources, we utilized these findings and found that, under the guidance of the Holy Spirit, they served to enrich our work:

My supervision time with Ms. Hernandez has improved my understanding of trauma, especially as it relates to the lives of my clients. Recently, I was discussing a client with Ms. Hernandez, and she helped me see how this client's severe trauma could be better understood by understanding how trauma affects the brain. We talked through Perry's study on neuropsychology, trauma, and the brain, and how this relates to the people [who] walk into our office. Although I have taken specific courses related to trauma in school, my supervision time has given me a first-hand look at how this trauma relates specifically to the people I work with. I better understand the various parts of the brain, what they do, and how trauma affects the different "jobs" of the brain. I am beginning to recognize why a client may act a certain way and what might be happening in their brain. Ms. Hernandez continues to teach me that understanding the brain is important, and it is necessary to know these scientific findings, but it all needs to be done through the lens of Christ's redeeming power and hope. Science can only take us so far, and we owe it to our clients to understand all we can about them and their situations in this respect, but Christ is the ultimate healer.[13]

12. Christine, email message to the author, February 18, 2014.
13. Marianne, email message to the author, February 19, 2014.

Church Feedback

At one church, we had the opportunity to conduct pre- and post-training analysis. We found it highly valuable in setting forth the material to be presented and in evaluating the impact of the training at its immediate conclusion and in the months following.

Although not everyone who completed the training participated in all the sessions, twenty-three people were issued certificates at the end of the program, with only one person having dropped out. We felt encouraged by the high attendance and the very low drop-out rate.

At the end of the twelve-week training, we asked all of the participants to complete a post-training survey, though ultimately only six completed this. A number of things stood out in the comments submitted. First, the participants clearly valued the opportunity to gain practical knowledge inside a biblical framework. They found the assigned reading helpful and claimed the training provided a growth experience. Also, they said that the instructor's love and compassion were evident. The most consistent suggestion for improvement from several of our participants was that future training programs should allow more time particularly for group discussion, role-playing exercises, case studies, and real-life examples.

One person expressed a wish for follow-up meetings after completion of the training to allow for this type of discussion and review. Unfortunately, we received minimal feedback regarding the various modules, which may be due to the fact that a good bit of time had elapsed since the presentation, making specific recollection understandably difficult. For organizations structuring training courses of this kind, the best time to gain information on each module is immediately following the presentation.

Evaluation from the City's Credentialing Agency

In January of 2013, the credentialing agency in Philadelphia conducted a comprehensive evaluation of the center's compliance with regulatory standards. They were so satisfied that they invited us to give a training in their seventh "Faith and Spiritual Affairs Conference." With two other leading psychologists, I gave a talk on "When to Turn It Off and Disconnect." Through this connection, I also became a member of a select group of interfaith individuals as a member of their Faith Advisory Board, offering guidance and input to the top leaders of the Department of Behavioral

Health and Intellectual Disability Services, leading in mental health services for the metropolitan area.

The Place of Refuge also conducted a self-appraisal in keeping with the core values set forth by DBHDS. It addressed the ways in which the agency adhered to those values in the domains of accessible care; individualized, person-first practices; an atmosphere that promotes strength, recovery and resilience; and supportive program operations and supervision.

In accordance with the agency's recommendation for improvement, the center initiated efforts in the following areas: development of a comprehensive trauma screening tool for assessment; a training plan on incorporation of faith-based principles; a detailed plan for creation of a peer program; a training/supervision policy based on guidelines for treatment plans, assessments, and notes; and a monthly quality assurance review to ensure that staff information is updated.

Institutional and State Feedback

While we recognized the significant outreach opportunity that a lay counseling training program could provide, we found it especially encouraging that the concept strongly supported the guidelines and goals set forth by the Philadelphia Behavioral Health Services Transformation model, the local regulatory agency that licensed and oversaw the work of the Place of Refuge.

The nine core values outlined in their document spoke directly to the goals of a lay counseling effort such as that of Refuge. In studying and working under the regulations put forth by this department, it became very clear that their guidelines fundamentally derived from—or at the very least, were significantly informed by—the beliefs and values of the Christian faith. Below, I outline briefly those nine core values listed in the document and their relevance to all of the various lay counseling efforts we undertook.

1. *Strength-based approaches that promote hope.* A lay counseling program focuses on building strength within the individual and family, bringing hope through the strengthening of the person's faith in Jesus Christ.

2. *Community inclusion, partnership, and collaboration.* The lay counseling program is built upon a partnership and collaboration with one of the chief community resources—the local parish.

3. *Person- and family-directed approaches.* Church attendance and membership is most frequently a family event. The lay counselor most

likely knows and is known by the family members of a suffering individual and can therefore bring the personal and family dynamic into the assessment and any possible treatment provided.

4. *Peer culture, support, and leadership.* The document states, "creating environments in which peers can support one another in formal and informal ways . . ." As a central component of lay counseling, this describes precisely what the lay counselor can and does do.

5. *Person-first (culturally competent) approaches.* The Place of Refuge's personnel and location stood in a unique position to address this key component as it applied to the large and growing Hispanic population within the city of Philadelphia, and increasingly in the rest of America. The principles also apply to other cultural groups. Through the lay counseling program and other speaking invitations, this core value was emphasized and supported.

6. *Trauma-informed approaches.* The recognition of trauma-based mental health issues has received wide attention in counseling circles. The lay counselor especially can "provide services in a safe and trustworthy environment through respectful, nurturing relationships that promote healing and avoid inadvertent re-traumatization."

7. *Holistic approaches toward care.* The lay counselor's approach is holistic—he or she sees suffering people within their community and cultural setting and can identify environmental, family, community, health-related, sexual, spiritual, and many other care issues.

8. *Care for the needs and safety of children and adolescents.* While the services of Refuge did not include a component of care specifically geared toward children and adolescents, the lay counselor trained using its model engages the individual within the family setting and is in a unique position to identify any child-specific issues and refer where needed.

9. *Partnership and transparency.* As evident throughout this book, the partnership established with the church community is at the core of any lay counseling relationship.[14]

14. More information on these goals can be accessed through the organization's website: https://dbhids.org.

How the Modules Help

As the Refuge teaching modules are the product of decades of practical and fruitful ministry, the training they offer can enhance any outreach, church, seminary, university program, or organization seeking to produce well-equipped workers to enter the chaos and pain of the world and bring the healing of Christ. If the Place of Refuge, for example, had had these complete modules during the early stages of its development, our ministry would have grown even stronger in various ways.

First, I believe our collaboration would have been powerful from the outset with Esperanza Health Center, local churches, and educational institutions. The Refuge model in its full form leads to boldness: especially boldness in offering the cultural competency module to Christian professionals who come to minister to the poor. Understanding culture and worldview is key to speaking the truth of the gospel to any people group.

I was reminded of this need one day as I met with a health provider of a local faith-based health center. This young man, originally from a Middle Eastern region, came to our center wracked with the effects of terrorism. During his time serving in his country's army, he worked as a paramedic, a first responder on the scene after suicide bombings, during which he developed PTSD. Ministering in North Philadelphia years later was rewarding to him on many counts, yet the adjustment to this new culture and its social dynamics triggered some of his PTSD symptoms, including hyper-arousal leading to anger, which drove him to seek counsel in our ministry.

One day, I asked him if I could use part of our session to share the module on Hispanic cultures and cultural competency. I believed this would clarify his thinking and would strengthen his desire to work in the city. He listened attentively and with much interaction as we exchanged our thoughts, comparing and contrasting between Hispanic cultures, his own culture, and that of historical Anglo-Saxon heritage. At the end of the session, he stated that his whole agency should receive this training and wondered why the leaders in his organization did not provide this information to all of their new hires as an integral part of the orientation and training. Weeks later, when we met, he admitted that he had experienced a growth of understanding and care, and that the anger he felt towards some of his patients was gone. Viewing his patients from their own cultural worldview and heritage freed him from misconceptions and misunderstandings. Understanding the cultural and sociological context enabled him to feel more empathy and compassion for those he served.

His experience reminds all of us that when we can enter into the invisible aspects of a person's inner life and worldview, we can share our faith more deeply, as many saints have had to learn in other lands. Hudson Taylor, founder of China Inland Mission, knew this all too well. He understood the significance faith played as we live out our lives, and he had to learn more about faith in his context when he crossed cultures to evangelize to the people of China: "We want a faith not loud, but deep, a faith not born of sentiment and human sympathy, but that comes from the vision of the living God."[15]

Second, if Refuge had had the full model from its inception, we would have been able to incorporate more interns earlier on (four per year, as opposed to only one for each of the first three years). Mentoring graduate students is a rewarding practice and an excellent method of bringing the new generation to our urban areas: a way for young disciples of Christ to show the church that they will follow God on God's terms and not on theirs. Having the complete training program would have exponentially increased our ability to orient new trainees and ready them quickly for service.

Third and finally, if I had had the wisdom we gained in those decades, I would have leaned more, as it were, on the richness found in each believer as the heart responds in obedience to Christ's commands and guidance. I have great respect for expert knowledge and education, and our work at the Place of Refuge would have been hampered immensely without the findings of modern science. The work of experts illuminates and informs what Christians do and have believed throughout the years, and often, their findings offer support of what we hold to be true. Yet I have learned that the cornerstone of excellent counseling is the sweetness and love of the hand reaching out, not only the professional credentials of the helper. As I have noted, all three leading mental health providers and researchers quoted in previous chapters (Herman, Bloom, and Perry) have said the same thing: transformative healing occurs within *relationship*, where people are safe and cared for with patience and wisdom. The pioneering work of Dr. Langberg highlights this truth with excellence.[16] The people of God can embody this patience, care, and wisdom in the earthen vessels of our lives and service.

The stories and case studies of this chapter, and the training modules outlined in the next, serve as a stepping-stone for multiplying the work of Christ among the marginalized. Whether through presentations, training

15. Broomhall, *Hudson Taylor*, 5.
16. Langberg, *Counseling*.

seminars, or other venues, application of this material will help raise up new waves of lay counselors from many walks of life, emboldened to come alongside those who have experienced suffering, those who are looking for hope and help. In this way, the diverse body of Christ becomes equipped to share the basic message of the gospel:

> The Spirit of the Lord is upon me,
> because he has anointed me
> to proclaim good news to the poor.
> He has sent me to proclaim liberty to the captives
> and recovering of sight to the blind,
> to set at liberty those who are oppressed,
> to proclaim the year of the Lord's favor. (Luke 4:18–19)

5

Making Refuge Spread

THE PLACE OF REFUGE, as it stands, can and does humbly hold up one small candle in one small corner of one small neighborhood, within a large city recognized as among the country's most needy. Those who have come to their door have received healing and will continue to do so in the years to come. However, Refuge's outreach efforts (through professional education and the lay counseling model) have taken that single candle and created a model for a radiance of God's love for the people of North Philadelphia—and, by extension, for many others in different parts of the world. By training others and expanding the vision through the inclusion of lay counselors, the model grew exponentially. While this expansion may not have been in our minds as a long-term plan, it was clearly in God's long-term plan.

This chapter offers guidance on how to establish lay counseling training and efforts within your own community, ministry, congregation, or organization, followed by an in-depth description of each training module of the Refuge model. These modules can act as a springboard for ministry efforts to be tailored to the unique needs represented in different communities.

How to Establish Lay Counseling in Your Organization

The following section outlines steps needed to establish a lay counseling program within a church or other agency. While this outline presents an ideal situation, each step should be considered and adapted to the needs and capabilities of the organization in question.

Pre-Training Assessment and Planning

The first and most critical step is to identify the decision-maker(s) within the establishment. Within many churches, things often do not happen if the lead pastor has not given approval to the project, though this may change by denominational or community polity. In an agency, whether its mission be secular or faith-based, support from top administration is essential. These individuals must be identified and their buy-in obtained before the organization initiates any planning. In conjunction with identifying these decision-makers, the next step is to have them create a leadership team. They will know their organization and its people best and are in a position to determine who and how many should make up that team. In many cases, the organization's primary leader(s) may have a team leader in mind; though alternatively, the team itself can pick its leader from within its own ranks, subject to the primary leadership approval.

Together, the organizational leaders and the lay counseling team can provide essential information regarding the cultural, economic, and health status of its members or its target population. They can provide input regarding the values of the community and faith (if applicable) of the members. From them, the trainer/consultant can piece together a detailed picture of the community with whom the lay counselors will be working, and (if possible) a survey can be administered to a population sample. All of this will help the trainer or consultant in the process of determining the tailored content of the program.

When the team has gathered sufficient formal and informal information, the trainer/consultant will be in a position to draw from a wealth of training information and training modules. With these materials, he or she will outline a draft version of the full training program. The Refuge model, which I provide later in this chapter, can be used as a loose framework for training, with adaptation to the target population in question as needed; it can also be used in its complete form as an exhaustive curriculum. Whatever the case, the trainer/consultant must carefully assess the training needs at hand, with the help of the team and the leadership, and make all program choices with care and intention.

Once the team is in place, the trainer/consultant must meet with them. This is a critical step in the planning process, because it is here that the team establishes rapport, building trust among themselves, sharing input, and cementing their commitment to work together. While subject to change, at this point, the trainer/consultant can usually give the team a clear estimation of the time commitment required for participating in training. If anyone on the team cannot make a definitive commitment to complete the training and to continue to function as a lay counselor, he or she should be given the opportunity, without judgment, to withdraw. It matters far more that all team members have a commitment from the heart that they will fulfill this ministry. Lay counseling requires certain knowledge and skills, but more importantly, it requires the mercy and compassion that Jesus Christ taught us to manifest as evidence of our faith—and that cannot be forced.

At this initial meeting, the trainer/consultant will share with the team the assessment information gathered to this point regarding the community and its needs. The team members will be given an opportunity to share their input as well. At the end of the first meeting, the trainer/consultant will ask the team to complete a pre-training survey, which will give further direction regarding the final design and goals of the training. The team will be told how many sessions will be held and what their duration will be, and they will also be shortly forwarded the dates, times, and place of the training. The trainer/consultant should, before the meeting's close, collect contact information for all members of the team, which should be made available to all course participants. After all, one of the goals of the training is to build a sense of camaraderie, and to encourage the members to support and encourage one another as they work.

While perhaps this may seem like a lot of pre-planning, it is nevertheless the most important part of a successful program. Without first establishing an infrastructure to support the project, it will not likely get off the ground. As we often found, in the lack of planning for longevity, trainees will finish the program inspired and excited but then will not know what to do with their inspiration, ultimately losing their momentum or burning out.

As quickly as possible (I suggest no more than two weeks), the complete program should be ready for presentation, and the team should hold a second meeting. Any additional input is welcome, of course; however, the trainer/consultant should bear in mind that the program's design already takes into account the larger picture of the community, input from the leadership, and feedback from the team. Individual trainees will have other ideas as well, but not every individual's ideas can be included.

If anyone on the team has special learning needs, the trainer/consultant can provide one-on-one time with that person, and/or outside resources to supplement their learning. At this final planning meeting, the team will have the confirmed dates, times, and location of the training.

Conducting the Training Program

By this time, the trainer is well prepared to conduct the sessions. He or she should ideally have all the training materials and any needed equipment and supplies available before the beginning of the first session. Depending on the length of the training, the trainer may want to bring in guest speakers who have expertise in a given area. A short evaluation questionnaire covering the learning objectives for that session should be distributed at the end of each gathering. It is helpful to let the trainees know that submitting these evaluations is a requirement of the course. The evaluations do not require a signature, but the monitor should check off that each form has been turned in as the trainees leave the room.

In addition, a final evaluation of the entire program should be administered at the close of the last session. This evaluation should mirror the questions asked in the pre-training survey. It will determine how well the trainer/consultant met the expressed learning needs of trainees.

Post-Training Activities

Before completing the training, the leadership team should meet with the trainer/consultant to plan and schedule how they will announce the availability of lay counseling service to the congregation and/or their target population. This plan of announcement methods can then be shared with the trainees at the last training session. By having such a plan in place, the trainees will have a sense of the organization's commitment to the project, will maintain the momentum built through training, and will enjoy the confidence that their new-found skills will be put to use rather than dropped. Accordingly, the organization then makes this announcement in an appropriate venue and in such a way that the recipients of the service understand what the lay counselors are doing and can prepare themselves to take advantage of what the counselors offer.

The leadership team, in conjunction with the trainer/consultant, needs to set up a system to document what occurs within the organization, including a feedback system from the lay counselors that should be presented in the last session. Many people do not like, or do not feel comfortable with, written documentation. The leadership team should keep this in mind and make provision for a feedback system that works for everyone. Even if the feedback from the lay counselors takes place in an informal manner, the team leader should ultimately have a written system to record the outcomes of their efforts.

Within the first month of announcing the program, the lay counselor should, along with the leadership and the trainer/consultant, provide feedback on the process to-date. They should at this time have an opportunity to express any questions or concerns they might have. If additional training is indicated, the leadership should schedule it as quickly as possible. If there are lay counselors who require individual supervision, the trainer/consultant can, in most situations, provide that. Depending on the needs of the organization or church, the trainer/consultant should make themselves available to the group for up to one year.

It is vitally important that the church or organization maintains regularly scheduled monthly meetings with the lay counseling team. The trainer/consultant will be available to help the team leader plan these meetings, or even attend the meetings, as needed. Experience showed us at the Place of Refuge that, without this kind of carefully planned infrastructure, a good idea and the best of intentions will soon fade and die.

A Word about Evaluation

While you do not want to burden the team with too much evaluating work, nevertheless, the process should not be overlooked. If possible, a survey conducted six months after the beginning of counseling work can provide valuable insight, guidance, and correctives to the program. This, in combination with a review of the team leader's documentation, should be presented to top administration in the form of a report, preferably written, for record-keeping purposes.

As stated above, this represents the ideal steps to take in establishing a program. Some organizations may not be able to do it to this level of detail. Any program will naturally be designed around the culture and capability of the organization in question, whether using the Refuge model without alterations, or a customized program informed by this model. Training topics and the manner of their presentation will be tailored to the learning styles of the trainees. One element, however, absolutely *cannot* be omitted if a program is to flourish and achieve lasting effect: the establishment of an infrastructure to support the work of the lay counselors. A leaderless program will not survive.

The Refuge Lay Counseling Training Model

The modules here outlined provide the lay counselor with a fundamental understanding of trauma, the potential risk of suicide, and the basic skills needed to be effective: listening, advocacy, relationship building, cross-cultural competency, and common pitfalls to avoid. For the faith-based organization, this material also includes the Christian principles of mercy and compassion.

In these learning modules, we strove to introduce lay counselors to many of the concepts and strategies that exist today in the world of the helping professions. We attempted to glean from the works of leading experts in the field in order to provide trainees with a well-rounded and contemporary foundation for their ministry. As such, much of the material we used in our training was not unique to the Place of Refuge, and the sources I have documented in sharing the training modules are all excellent material for further study.

Finally, in the development and growth of a lay counseling program, the particular learning/training needs of the group will emerge. It is in this spirit that I offer the Refuge lay counseling model as a springboard, a starting point, and a guiding framework for the tailored work of a given ministry to a specific demographic or community.

Why These Modules?

The Theology Behind the Modules

In developing each module, our primary theological guide was the image of God and the *shalom* God aims to bring into the heart of each individual. God does not desire that we live in chaos, depression, or despair—rather, God wants to bring healing in the midst of suffering.

In the same way God came and took on flesh like us, our ministries must seek to be *incarnational* and *relational*. Thus, the modules on cultural competency, understanding trauma, and so forth all help the counselor to enter the place of suffering alongside those who are hurting. And in the modules on listening skills, bereavement, and building relationships, we strengthen the counselor's relational capabilities. Even our modules that heavily use modern psychological and scientific discovery (such as the module on trauma, or the module on the parameters of lay counseling) ultimately look to Christ's healing power for our guidance and our hope. When developing each module, we aimed to ground the training in a christological and biblical approach.

We ultimately concluded that, for a culture with a long history of poverty (as most postcolonial Hispanic cultures have), these modules seem to fit. The people struggled to hold on to their own culture in an entirely new country, having to navigate their faith, work ethic, and family life as the *other* in a larger culture that did not speak their native tongue and shared precious few cultural institutions. The social manner in majority-culture society, unlike the warm and hospitable atmosphere of home, was now formal and distantly professional. The new immigrant found himself or herself an alien, a displaced person—in other words, a sojourner or a pilgrim: familiar concepts, if the person is a Christian. As such, the eight Refuge modules had great impact, at least as a start. Emphasizing the life and death of Christ, and above all the *shalom* of God, fits as a theological framework.

Module One: The Parameters of Lay Counseling

Overview

We crafted this module as the beginning of the lay counseling training to set boundaries between lay counseling and professional clinical work. We did not want to cause any harm to people suffering from their relationships, and in order to avoid this, it was crucial to make a line of demarcation between *lay* and *professional* counseling, and their two distinct levels of purpose and aims. The lay counselor needs to understand the limits of this helping relationship and to discern when to refer someone for professional treatment. Hence, in our objectives, we set the structure clearly.

Special attention was given to emotional involvement, as wisdom had taught us that nothing can ruin the building of a trusting and safe relationship as much as an unhealthy emotional involvement between the helper and the sufferer.

Objectives

- To demonstrate an understanding of how lay counseling differs from what the professional clinician does.
- To develop an understanding of what the lay counselor can do.
- To develop the prerequisite skills required by the lay counselor.
- To establish healthy boundaries within lay counseling dimensions.

Content

Spirituality in the Mental Health Field

The recent embrace of people of faith and their input as a significant factor in life is transforming the way our culture sees mental health care. I would offer two examples: 1) The American Psychological Association's Department of Religion and Psychology, focusing on spirituality and counseling; and 2) the city of Philadelphia and the state of Pennsylvania's choice to give the Place of Refuge credentialing as a faith-based, specialty center. It had, according to city authorities, filled a gap for the many people who seek a faith-based alternative to the mainstream mental health model. In prior years, such acceptance within the mental health field might not have come about.

Filling the Gap: Lay Counseling Versus Professional

Today's Health Maintenance Organizations (HMOs) require professional helpers to work out of an economic model that limits the length of therapy.[1] One ray of hope for the hurting, however, remains unchanged: Christians, in a lay capacity, have more resources and freedom in this area and can fill this gap. The Holy Spirit of God, with the truth, compassion, and mercy found in the gospel of Jesus Christ, offers solutions to life's demands and suffering. Believers possess a practical theology: common sense coupled with a theological understanding of the human condition, which are both inseparable elements of true helping. Even the Christian who lacks professional training can learn to listen to the struggles of people and lessen their burdens thereby. Lay counselors are burden-bearers. After all, only a small

1. Kennedy and Charles, *On Becoming*, vii.

percentage of people seek professional counseling. One can still respond effectively to the anxious or troubled person who seeks assistance.

Who Does the Helping?

"We are all much more simply human than anything else," psychiatrist Harry Stack Sullivan once observed.[2] An acceptance and appreciation of our shared brokenness or limits is the greatest strength of a counselor. We all have a special "treasure in earthen vessels" (2 Cor 4:7 KJV), an account that we can never overdraw. Doctors, lawyers, teachers, hair-stylists, and so many others—including congregants within the church—have people who come to and confide in them, turning the unsuspecting person into a counselor. Hurting people bring their problems to others looking for understanding or common sense, even when they disguise the first hints of emotional pain. These situations can be difficult for the untrained individual to navigate.

What Helpers Can Do

The person with common sense or wisdom (what I would call *spiritual intelligence*) can use even a few minutes redemptively. "They help by simply being human with the troubled other, by managing the resources of their own spirits, and capitalizing on the strength of their best instincts"[3]—the life of Christ in them—to reply to the need. These resources can come to their aid when navigating the stress that sharing someone else's pain can cause. After all, a counseling ministry can be a very rewarding experience, yet it can also be highly stressful, because counselors work one-on-one with the greatest stress producer we know—other people. In light of this, therefore, "Helpers must monitor and identify their own reactions, or these reactions will hijack them."[4] In other words, taking care of one's self is part of taking care of others. As others like Kennedy have noted, what proves healthy in the helper is usually more reliable than the advice of the most well-known psychologist.

2. Kennedy and Charles, *On Becoming*, viii.
3. Kennedy and Charles, *On Becoming*, ix.
4. Kennedy and Charles, *On Becoming*, ix.

The Helper's Humanity

Not everyone can go to a professional for help. A significant portion of counseling happens when the average person tries to answer questions such as: "How do we move on beyond this?" "How can I stop worrying?" or, "I need to forgive, but how?" At times, you can refer people to someone trained in the field—but what can you do in the meantime, or when referral is impossible? What should you provide in the event of the death of someone's spouse or child, for which there is no easy reassurance or cure? "Sometimes you have no choice; human situations arise without warning,"[5] and so preparedness ahead of time can make the difference between fumbling and helping.

This training encourages lay counselors who want to improve their ability to work effectively with others. As a person and as a Christian, the lay counselor can stand next to those who suffer, using her basic strengths, good judgment, and availability. Our model provides a way to acquire sufficient skills to respond to emotional problems with concern for others and respect for one's own limitations. The better-trained the lay counselor, the more the feelings of being overwhelmed in the face of pain will dissolve.

Emotional Involvement

Non-professionals do a substantial amount of supportive counseling. In light of this fact, "we must guard against the inappropriately informal relationships that have become the style today."[6] If the counselor becomes too available, emailing and texting can confuse the boundaries that ought to be in place. Even though "traditionally, professional counseling began in a cold, distant, sterile environment,"[7] and over time, casual relationships (e.g., patients calling their therapists by first name) became the norm, we should recognize that there is a risk involved here: "This pretend-intimacy is a further example of the political democratization of counseling that undermines professional standards and insights."[8] Some form of boundary should be maintained, in order to protect the lay counselor from overwhelming involvement in someone else's troubles.

5. Kennedy and Charles, *On Becoming*, x.

6. Kennedy and Charles, *On Becoming*, xii.

7. Kennedy and Charles, *On Becoming*, xiii.

8. Kennedy and Charles, *On Becoming*, xiii.

These troubles bring up responses in us we do not always anticipate. There can be great stress involved in counseling another person. These emotions sometimes go unidentified, but they nevertheless affect us deeply, and one could get absorbed in them. Becoming emotionally compromised can weaken the lay counselor's composure and severely limit his ability to help. When this happens, sooner or later, the lay counselor will want to escape the mess.

To help avoid this, our training offers resources for reflection and self-evaluation that help counselors remain personal and involved without fearing that they will inevitably be lost in the process.

What We Can Do for Others

In many ways, this question drives people whose passion is to help. While helpers want to offer constructive aid to people in distress, we don't always know how to do so. In most emotional problems, however, a little help serves as a lot.

Lay counselors need honest and reasonable expectations about what they can accomplish in their counseling. They should not feel badly when they cannot "fix" people—not even professional counselors can do that. "There is honor, however, in helping persons to move even a few inches closer to self-responsibility, in assisting them to turn to a new and healthier direction in life."[9] When we manage our expectations, aiming not for a whole-life fix, but for that "few inches" of progress, we stand a greater chance of longevity and usefulness in lay counseling:

> The curse in the soul of "amateur" therapists is their determination to change people at all costs. And they frequently blunder, trampling on the sacred places of others' personalities in the process. The lay counselor must be encouraged to learn to deliver a service that is solid and lasting, even though it is a small beginning. Understanding is at the heart of all good therapy. It transmits through the discipline of counseling skills, clarity, and it helps bewildered people to see themselves in better perspectives.[10]

9. Kennedy and Charles, *On Becoming*, xiv.
10. Kennedy and Charles, *On Becoming*, xiv.

Module Two: A Theological Framework

Overview

Our objectives here were to provide the lay counselor with a basic understanding of the theology behind our training and to provide tools for spiritual assessment and care. Since the center was faith-based, we focused on the *shalom* of God as a biblical theme; our training explicitly helped counselors to create an environment in which the client can experience the *shalom* of God and its transformative, healing power. We did stress, however, that counselors should not proselytize or forcefully insist on making spirituality a focus of counseling. Many people recovering from great trauma have understandable wariness (even hatred) toward God, and only the experience of God's gentle *shalom* can help the person soften toward spiritual matters. In such situations, we instruct the counselor to let the client initiate spiritual questioning and requests for spiritual care.

Objectives

- To give the lay counselor an understanding of the theology behind counseling in trauma and our role as shepherd-helpers to the hurting.
- To provide the counselor with tools for spiritual assessment and treatment.

Content

Framework for Our Model

A Christian counseling center seeking to help bring redemption and transformation to the inner city must be, from its very foundations, incarnational and relational. Refuge's counselors and social workers provided the presence of Christ through the embodiment of the Holy Spirit, which their clients from North Philadelphia experienced in repeated meetings. When those clients returned home with the experience of God, their family situations began to change as the individuals worked with the center's professionals. This offered a multiplication effect of new life and godliness. As Dr. Langberg teaches,

We are called into the places of darkness and death, for that is where He went. He has called us to serve Him in this dark place of death, moving among those who are dead in their trespasses and sin, calling them to life and light. The church is called to bring the holiest of things alongside acts of mercy in a devastated place.[11]

Building a counseling relationship with hurting people involves a "walking with" through the fallen and burned out places of their souls, and an engagement with their culture, respecting their human dignity and God's image in them. Relationship can only occur when each party knows they are accepted and known, without criticism or judgment.

Genuine love in the Hispanic community takes a different form in professional spheres than it does in mainstream mental health care. For many Hispanics, acts of respect and genuine connection are based on a clear message of culturally appropriate expressions of warmth.

Socially acceptable professional Christian behavior therefore includes physical expressions of care and concern. Establishing rapport, from the perspective of the individual, will mean that you become part of his or her extended family. This can create problems for a counselor: food and gifts are common gestures in this culture, and the professional counselor finds herself in a bind if she chooses to follow the ethical professional boundaries between client and counselor that dictate that she may receive no gifts. A lay counselor, however, operates with greater freedom. He or she can learn how to use professional training to minister in meaningful ways within a cultural context, beyond the standards of the profession.

In addition, Christian counseling champions the Lord's *justice*. The counselor at times must speak with the voice of the Lord, standing against evil, deception, corruption, false doctrine, and discrimination, speaking both into the life of the individual and into the systems that bring on suffering and deep-seated problems to the poor. The Word of God becomes the instrument of truth. Counselors form solidarity with individuals in overcoming the effects of injustice; they work together to confront the wrong in these people's lives. Sometimes this confrontation leads to rebellion and rejecting God's truth; for others, it leads to reconciling suffering and finding God's way out of their dilemmas. The counselor models God's justice to each person, serving as the bridge between that person and God,

11. Dr. Langberg presented this idea to me during a supervisory meeting in early 2004.

and offering a new way of seeing reality. This act can give the impetus for transforming expectations of how God might work in other areas of life.

Christianity by its nature is didactic. To offer a tutorial to others, learning to follow in the way of Christ in the inner city, the center took on a sacred task. We derived all teaching from the character of God. Our blueprint for life and godliness was a learned discipline, and therefore, training younger multicultural therapists and social workers made up a crucial part of the center's calling. To that end, Refuge offered layers of teaching about urban issues and clinical psychology for growth and maturity in the younger generation, modeling that maturity and skill, training in clinical insights to urban problems, and training in diagnoses and symptoms.

We also incorporated teaching into the counseling setting. While working with the clients, internal wounds encompassed the bulk of their souls' preoccupation. Because of the discipling nature of this work, the inner confrontation of God's truths became tangible, though often hard for them to grasp initially. Their growth in understanding was the process of healing which brought maturity to themselves and their outlook.

The Shalom of God

Obedience to God is the greatest fact of life, having the potential to revolutionize all of our relationships. To be rightly related to God means that we join in a covenant relation of "a divinely established relationship of union and communion between God and his people in the bonds of mutual love and faithfulness."[12] The fruit of this mutual love between God and humans is known as *shalom*. Wolterstorff writes: "In *shalom*, each person enjoys justice, enjoys his or her rights. There is no *shalom* without justice."[13] We see an important part of God's *shalom* within incarnational relationships formed with those who have suffered from great injustice. Within the people of God and counseling, *shalom* means that we enter into the dark places of souls to bring comfort, compassion, love, and the sustaining power of faith and hope.

12. Shepherd, "Law and Gospel," 73.
13. Wolterstorff, *Until Justice*, 69.

Shalom as More than the Absence of Hostility

The *shalom* of God within the greater context of the urban church is one of the most important ways to witness to the world. *Shalom* transforms people once socially marginalized, victimized from injustices through economic disparity and other systemic evils, and brings them to their peace in God. After all, the church is composed of former enemies of God, reconciled to God and to each other through the death and resurrection of Christ.

Although originally incompatible, the people in the church now make up a new covenantal people, forming bonds with each other through the *shalom* of God. Reversing the effects of former alienation from God and with each other, the people of God now display God's *shalom* as they go out into their communities with the message of peace. To the outside world, the church becomes the open door into the sweet aroma of God's *shalom*, which transfigures the Hispanic church and community in the urban context. As Hispanics come to a real knowledge of God through the preaching of the word and through counseling, they too take up their roles within the kingdom of God.

Spiritual Consideration in the Assessment Process

The Place of Refuge, as a non-partisan, non-profit organization, answered to the guidelines and mandates of the Philadelphia Department of Behavioral Health and Intellectual Disabilities Services. As such, we were required to show how client assessments related to their spiritual beliefs. We answered this by describing the "Four P's."

1. *Precipitating.* A tragic event may have triggered an individual to question God, which often plays into the current behavioral concern or challenge.

2. *Perpetuating.* If an individual believes God rewards good and punishes bad, he may feel his current struggles are a punishment. This belief could perpetuate his feelings of depression, anxiety, or other troubles.

3. *Predisposing.* Spiritual beliefs an individual has had since childhood may affect her interpretation of the world. The counselor must gain understanding of the individual's worldview to effectively reach her.

4. *Protective.* Spiritual views or faith can serve as a protective factor when struggling with depression, anxiety, or other life challenges.

Religious and Spiritual Practices as Therapeutic Interventions[14]

Prayer

The counselor may pray silently, or vocally with the individual of faith, and the individual is encouraged to pray outside of the counseling situation. However, a counselor must use consideration: prayer cannot substitute for professional competency, and it may be appropriate with some clients and not with others. If a client has religious trauma in their background, initiating prayer could do more harm than good, especially as the counselor must take care not to impose his or her beliefs on the client. Prayer between a counselor and client must always happen with the client's consent!

Contemplation/Meditation

This practice is often used for individuals with stress-related problems: anxiety, depression, panic attacks, adjustment disorder, or PTSD. As with prayer, the type of meditation and contemplation suggested must be consistent with the individual's beliefs.

Reading Sacred Writings

Sacred writings might include quoted scriptures, interpreted scriptures, indirect references, stories, memorization, and suggested readings and studies. This tactic has been used successfully in challenging dysfunctional beliefs. However, the counselor should not set herself up as an authority on Scripture, nor engage in debates.

Forgiveness and Repentance

Encouraging forgiveness is one of the most frequently used interventions—but also a frequently *mis*used intervention, if the individual is not ready to forgive. The counselor should carefully consider the timing of the suggestion. Individuals may need to forgive parents, leaders of the church, or others who have hurt or abused them. Whatever the case, the counselor

---

14. The categories for this closer look at religious-spiritual interventions, which we utilized at the Place of Refuge and in our training, were developed by Richards and Bergin, *Spiritual*, 202–21.

should encourage individuals to be patient with themselves. Forgiveness is a long spiritual and emotional process, not a one-time event.

In conjunction with this, *repentance* "can be viewed as a prelude to forgiveness; that is, in repentance, people seek forgiveness from God, or from those they have hurt or offended, and it includes reform in thought, feeling, and action."[15]

Worship and Ritual

Worship helps when struggling with many challenges: questions of identity or purpose in life, loss and grief, major changes, and more. As an intervention, though perhaps not as frequently used, worship can offer much healing. The counselor may utilize a variety of therapeutic elements: music, liturgy and rituals, beautiful surroundings, and so forth. In this setting, the individual expresses devotion, love, appreciation, or even contrition.

Fellowship and Service

Here the lay counselor can play a key role in the therapeutic process. Offering fellowship and support can strengthen the individual spiritually, give her a sense of connectedness, and help her cope with stress, death, disease, or trauma. The lay counselor can encourage her to become involved in service herself, which will help her to avoid excessive self-preoccupation.

Seeking Spiritual Direction

Here again, the lay counselor (working, perhaps, with a lay leader or professional therapist) can play a key role in providing spiritual direction and its benefits (i.e., increased growth, absolution for guilt and shame, coping with challenges, and social support and acceptance). When therapy is complete, the lay counselor can provide support to maintain the progress made in therapy.

15. Richards and Bergin, *Spiritual,* 212.

Module Three: Building a Relationship, Understanding, and Trust

Overview

This module could not be overlooked or taken for granted; it takes skills to develop a relationship as a lay leader. Though one may believe, at the outset, that relationship building is a matter of common sense, in actuality we cannot undertake such a work merely with our natural affinities. Rather, we need to be thoughtful and purposeful—especially when entering a counseling relationship. Teaching participants the skills and pitfalls of relationship building served as a good start, but we also encouraged helpers to examine their motivations for building relationships. Building relationships is serious work; human life is sacred, and ministry is as well. The place of suffering in the human heart is a place of great vulnerability, and the potential for damage here is likewise great. No one should attempt to enter such a relationship lightly or for compromised reasons.

Objectives

- To develop the skills needed to build supportive relationships with parishioners seeking counseling.
- To demonstrate an understanding of the techniques for building supportive relationships.

Content

Some things should be avoided until the counselor has established a sufficient relationship. Intense questioning and probing should not be used at the outset, and until the counselor has a clear picture of the person's values, it is important to measure what is said. Naturally, some things we learn in counseling can only be learned through experience. Many times, we make mistakes before we can truly learn how to nurture people.

Listen to the Person

When people come to us, they do everything they can, often through incredible honesty, to help us learn who they are: they try to make better counselors out of us. After all, when they come to us, they come in a stance of meekness, sharing how life hurts them at a given moment or a given period of time. We practice listening to people not only through their words, but also through their nonverbal communication.[16]

Thinking of a person in terms of his problems often gets in the way of true listening. By listening, you communicate not your agreement that the events described were right or wrong, but rather that you understand he experienced them in this way. Forget about problems; think instead of the person experiencing the problems. The more we concentrate on the problem, the more we run the risk of missing the *person* in front of us.

We do not have to solve problems. We only have to help others accept that responsibility for themselves. The physician does not look at an organ without understanding its function and connection to the whole body. Similarly, we look at whole human beings and their reactions to the particular stressors of their lives. Unless we can manage to see the situation they describe, we will not get a good view of the phenomena we call "problems." When we operate free of responsibility to solve the problems of others, listening to the whole person, people can communicate uninhibited the strengths and supports they need in order to find solutions for themselves.

Don't Try to "Do Good"[17]

"Do-gooders" act on others only in response to their own needs. Doing good for others, of course, is not a bad thing. But we err when we set out with a purpose to impose good on a person at all costs. In helping situations, we naturally want the outcome of our efforts to bring goodness to other people. We only accomplish this, however, as a *by-product* of our sincere interest and our effective understanding of the person in front of us. "Trouble arises when we directly and sometimes unilaterally decide what must be done and how best to achieve our pre-planned outcome."[18] This approach is called

16. Cheydleur, *Called*, 30.
17. Kennedy and Charles, *On Becoming*, 24.
18. Kennedy and Charles, *On Becoming*, 25.

Rescue Fantasy, "a deep need to rearrange people's lives and to provide them with happy endings, designed by the counselor herself."[19]

Ask yourself, "What do I accomplish for others when I decide what they should or should not do? Whose needs are being met in this situation?"[20] These are difficult, but good, questions: if only to avoid the enormous stress and complicated emotions tied to such an arrangement. By participating in a rescue fantasy, we make it more difficult for the other person to take serious responsibility for her decisions. We don't do people a favor when we try to protect them from the consequences of their own actions, when we override their own wisdom and insights to favor our own, *or* when we deny them the opportunity to fail.[21]

What can we do? *We can guide them to find their own strength.* As Christians, we do not aim to impose goodness on others' lives; we must aim instead to strengthen their relationship with Christ, so they can confront and deal with their own lives effectively. Do not approach a hurting person with the breezy assumption that you have the answers. Take time to learn how to understand the person. Take time to learn the skills to identify strengths and natural resources in him. But also learn to not cross the line. Self-restraint acknowledges and respects the potential of others to gradu ally bring order into the confusion and chaos of their lives.

What can we give? We can give time, understanding, and our honest selves; but if we go beyond that, it can be quite harmful, especially if it comes out of our need to "do good" and "fix" people. The more honest we can be about this, the greater the potential to do *real* good.

Don't Try to Do Well

In doing well, our emphasis is on our own performance. We look at people as another task or test by which we can prove ourselves—our skill as a counselor, our wisdom, the quality of our insight—rather than seeing the person as a person. Trying to do well can be equally as destructive as trying to do good by imposing our own agenda.

The high achiever must take care here: the deep desire to perform admirably can interfere with helping others. Often, this motivation to do well goes so deep that it clouds our vision of life (especially of someone

19. Kennedy and Charles, *On Becoming*, 25.

20. Kennedy and Charles, *On Becoming*, 25.

21. Kennedy and Charles, *On Becoming*, 26.

else's life). Then we begin to see human beings as opportunities for personal achievements, rather than seeing people as individuals in themselves.[22] Less self-regard and more simple humanity make for good counseling.

Common Techniques in a Supportive Relationship

Guiding Principles Before Learning the Basic Skills

Some fundamental principles will guide the lay counselor in the right direction from the outset: 1) knowing one's own greatest strengths (in other words, understanding one's fundamental identity); 2) developing sensible supportive assistance by staying within boundaries and avoiding entanglements; and 3) maintaining respect for the person's coping mechanisms by identifying and reinforcing that person's defenses.

As a caring person, the counselor can help individuals explore their problems, providing clarification and suggestions. Most people need reassurance that their experiences are normal for human beings. Whenever appropriate, counseling can incorporate an educational component here, whether in the form of literature or simply through sharing personal experience.

Distinguishing Empathy and Sympathy

Relationships consist of reciprocal exchange. What the person feels and what he expresses constitutes his reality. As people speak, we listen; as they share, we feel, and vice versa. We must feel something. If we do not experience sympathy in response to someone's story of pain, we do not have enough passion to make a difference in that person's life. Without feeling, we can have no relationship.

There are, however, two kinds of feeling in this context: sympathy and empathy. To have sympathy means to understand another's plight; empathy is to actually *feel* what he feels. Too much empathy will soon drown the lay counselor. However, the capacity for sympathy will preserve one's strength to stay afloat. Keep in mind the saying that "you need not experience drowning to be a good lifeguard."

In helping the lay counselor learn to manage emotional involvement and maintain sympathy, we use in our training the following list of

22. Kennedy and Charles, *On Becoming*, 28.

questions designed by Kennedy and Charles to self-evaluate within the counseling relationship.

Mindful Questions for Counselors[23]

- What is behind my more-than-average interest in this person?
- What am I trying to get out of this relationship that I would not like to admit to myself?
- Am I always ready to argue with this person . . . or always ready to agree?
- Am I beginning to feel for this person?
- Do I think about him or her between sessions? Do I daydream about this person? If so, why?
- Do I feel bored when I am with him or her? Who makes it so—I, or the other?
- Do I overreact to statements the other person makes?
- Is there a reason that either of us is always late?
- Is there a reason that either of us wants more time together than we agreed upon?
- Why do I say this is the best (or the worst) person I ever worked with?
- Do I find myself wanting to end this relationship [early], or hold on to it even though it should come to an end?

Module Four: Listening Skills

Overview

In this module, we challenged helpers to understand the significance of listening with skill and intention, not only through verbal communication, but also through non-verbal. As with relationship building, people often think that listening is something everyone knows how to do naturally, something that does not require practice, thought, or improvement. This, however, is not the case. Listening skills take time to grow, require practice

---

23. Kennedy and Charles, *On Becoming*, 18.

and intentionality, and can be improved as we undergo training. This skill of listening well is a universal need to develop in life, but it becomes the case especially as we walk alongside a hurting person. One cannot counsel at any level if one does not listen to what the person says. During this training we did role-playing in groups of three (observer, helper, and person seeking help) and group exercises with the aim to give participants honest feedback.

Objectives

- To demonstrate the ability to listen to non-verbal communication.
- To demonstrate listening skills.

Content

Another Way of Listening

In the counseling relationship, we listen for clarification, for clearing away confusion in the individual. Normally, we think of listening as hearing what people say verbally, paying attention only to the words and content. At times, however, this kind of listening—while good—is not enough. Instead, "We listen in a new and indirect manner: listening to the non-verbal communication, looking at the symbolic language of the body."[24]

In doing this, we must trust our instinctive reactions to what we hear in words and body language. When confusion arises, we should take the time to hear that person, paying attention to her non-verbal cues as well as her words, and proceeding mindful of our own reactions to her. Confusion can result in inaccurate interpretations or self-destructive reactions, as when, for example, missed clues put the counselor at the mercy of an individual's emotional manipulation: she starts controlling and guiding *me* as the counselor, and I lose my capacity to help.

Instead, we can learn to not take things personally if we step away from the situation and ask, "What is it that I'm feeling?" Sometimes, these feelings shed light on the realities at hand. This gives us the opportunity to use otherwise destructive, overwhelming emotions as tools to understand and work with the person.

24. Kennedy and Charles, *On Becoming*, 31.

In other words, the messages that others deliver to us in a variety of ways during counseling reveal how others affect us. In response to someone's sharing, we may feel helpless, angry, frightened, or depressed. The ordinarily happy person feeling these things in the face of someone's story is receiving a first-hand experience of what others feel in relationship with the person. In this way, our own reactions to that person will further understanding and inform the ongoing relationship.[25]

For example, imagine that an otherwise professional, mature woman enters into a counseling relationship. The counselor does not realize the woman sees him as a surrogate parent, expecting parental care. As she transfers her helplessness to the counselor, soon he may feel overburdened and desirous of cutting off the relationship.

If he "listens" to this desire, he realizes that—despite the woman's credentials and self-presentation—she is a dependent personality: submissive, timid, and clingy. Some people take on a helpless role with everyone in this way, and they introduce trouble into many of their close relationships by demanding what others cannot give. The counselor experienced that pattern in the woman's life and intuitively reacted to it. The helplessness of a dependent personality can overwhelm, until we can immunize ourselves by becoming aware of how this process can and does operate—and this is only possible through listening.

Listening Skills: Skill-Building Group Exercise[26]

Listen for the Opportunity to Walk Alongside Another

Suppose a fellow parishioner approaches and makes a statement that indicates a reaching out, a request for help—however indirect. Many people let these moments pass. Yet with practice, we can instead learn to recognize that these moments provide an opportunity to walk with the sufferer. They may sound as non-committal as, "Excuse me, do you have a minute?" or as overt as, "Everybody around here treats me like a machine." Perhaps the statement is as suggestive as: "I want you to know that I would never say anything bad about my husband, but . . ." We ask trainees to listen for these

---

25. Kennedy and Charles, *On Becoming*, 32.

26. Our training also outlines these listening skill-building techniques developed by Cheydleur, *Called*, 30–38.

phrases or statements as an opportunity for counseling, and once heard, to identify a response approach.

Finding a Probe or Prompt

We always seek to respect the process that brought the individual to counseling. Sometimes she knows the instigating factors herself; at other times, the counselor must search for more understanding. Prayer and the Holy Spirit will provide more discernment. But in addition to this, we ask trainees to write down a "probe or prompt" statement, such as: "I have finally decided to separate from my husband." The counselor would then ask the person to respond to that sentence. Other prompts might be, "Do you think I am too old to go back to college?" or, "If God loves me, why would he allow this person to assault me?"

Developing Sensitivity

The lay counselor must avoid making personal judgments, to set aside her personal response and listen to the individual's feelings. We must validate what he expresses, mirroring back his feelings. We use the following exercise for working on this listening skill.

In response to each of the following statements, we ask trainees to restate, using an "I hear you saying that you feel . . . and" statement, both the emotion and content of the person:

- "I can't stand it anymore!" (*Sample restatement: "I hear you saying that you feel overwhelmed, and emotionally distressed."*)

- "My relationship is going better than I have a right to expect." (*"I hear you saying that you feel surprised, and satisfied."*)

- "I cannot do one more thing right now. I am a little frazzled around the edges." (*"I hear you saying that you feel exhausted, and a bit anxious."*)

- "You're the only person who has shown me some caring in this whole rotten mess." (*"I hear you saying that you feel cared for, and that you're in a very complicated situation."*)[27]

27. Statements from Cheydleur, *Called,* 33. Sample responses are my own.

Timing

Timing can be very important—both to seize the moment and to allow enough time and space for good interaction. Impromptu counseling situations have three layers: the individual's need, the time needed, and the counselor's concern and response. Let us say a man approaches the lay counselor in the church parking lot, just before service begins, and says, "I'm so upset about what's happening to my daughter. I've just got to talk to someone about it today. I'm really terrified, and I don't know what to do!" The counselor now has a clear opportunity to walk alongside this man, but the timing is inopportune. How should one respond?

We asked trainees to identify the parishioner's feelings, the counselor's feelings, and the time available. They had to try to combine the reflection of the individual's content, a statement of time available, and the counselor's emotional and spiritual concern into an appropriate response, which could look something like this:

> "I see the need that you have, and my heart goes out to you, but service will be starting in five minutes. Can you sit with me in the conference hall for those five minutes? I don't want you to feel that I don't care for you, because I really do. If we can sit together now, we can schedule some time later so you can have my undivided attention."

Practicing Give and Take

In response to the following statement, we asked trainees to reflect on content (what they thought); to identify emotions (what they felt); and to list values (what they believed). "When I dropped out of the seminary, I felt terrible because I thought God had deserted me, even though I was happy. I was marrying the girl of my dreams. All my friends told me I was doing the right thing."[28] Give and take comes when, instead of just listening, the counselor rephrases the content and emotions she has just heard. This protects her from getting ahead of the individual and giving premature advice before she truly understands what he is saying.

---

28. Cheydleur, *Called*, 38.

Module Five: Understanding Trauma and Its Impact

Overview

I have already discussed in great detail in chapter 3 how trauma is not only an area of specialty in the discipline of psychology, but also how the process of recovery requires cultural competency as an integral part of healing. We sensed early on that understanding how different cultures respond to trauma and its implications would strengthen our help to the sufferer. We knew that a training program would not be complete without an understanding of cultural competency, as discussed above. But we also knew that our staff would need a thorough understanding of trauma—and that not in the abstract, but as illuminated within the context of culture. Our training needed to include both components, since each would inform the other. For this reason, we developed the training module on trauma, both for our interns and staff, and ultimately for the lay counselors as well.

This module on trauma held great significance for our target population in another way. Time and again, we discovered that behind the diagnosis of depression, anxiety, or other psychosomatic disorders lay a history of early childhood sexual abuse. Sometimes, we learned that a client may have had one incident of molestation. For others, it occurred multiple times. Worse yet, for some clients, sexual abuse may have been chronic and by multiple perpetrators. Sadly, in our community, we knew that the two individuals who most commonly perpetrated the abuse were step-fathers and grandfathers. In my two decades of counseling, I found—and data consistently backed up my personal findings—that clients were rarely abused by strangers; most abusers were family members, extended family members, or friends (in Hispanic culture, such relationships often become regarded as equivalent to *familia*).

Even a brief survey of new developments in the discipline of psychology today makes apparent the all-encompassing discussion taking place regarding trauma. Trauma has now become a part of our lexicon, and we are all drawn into a better understanding of its nature. The church of Christ and Christian psychologists are taking notice, as exemplified in the existence of the Global Trauma Institute at Biblical Theological Seminary, led by my colleagues Dr. Philip Monroe and Dr. Langberg. In ministering to the church of Jesus Christ, we will meet many who have this kind of suffering.

Objectives

- To provide participants with a basic understanding of the nature of trauma, its signs, and its impact.
- To familiarize participants with the course of treatment undertaken with the trauma patient.
- To provide participants with an understanding of, and skills to advocate for, people suffering from trauma.

Content

Trauma and Its Impact

As we have explored in previous chapters, trauma takes place when an event instills terror or helplessness in the victim. Trauma experiences shake the foundations of the victim's beliefs about safety, shattering assumptions about trust. Trauma may be a one-time event or repetitive events in the person's life. It may manifest in different ways: hyper-arousal resulting in stress, anxiety, and vigilance; reliving/re-experiencing in the form of flashbacks, nightmares, intrusive thoughts, and triggers; and/or numb withdrawal through dissociation (going through the motions but not being present), or amnesia. Trauma damages relationships, creates relational shame, and distorts the self, identity, and personhood. The terror experienced with trauma differs from biological fear in that it rewires the brain, so that even after the event is over, the person responds as if it were still happening.[29]

In many ways, we are not the same people when terrified as when calm. Our bodies change in a remarkable way as perceptual abilities, emotional states, thought processes, attention, and memory all shift in response to trauma. We become, in some senses, another person—no longer able to respond to others as we would under less threatening circumstances.[30]

We all have a "volume control" over our level of arousal (internal anxiety, fear, or alertness). However, people severely or repeatedly traumatized lose this control, the capacity to modulate their level of arousal. They stay

29. Herman, *Trauma*, 33.
30. Bloom, *Sanctuary*, 15.

hyper-aroused and guarded, unable to calm themselves even when they see the danger has passed.[31]

Reactions to trauma manifest in many ways, whether in thought or action, physical or spiritual. Even physical responses can vary a great deal. Some reactions to trauma and their possible manifestations include: panic, paranoia, dry mouth, nightmares, confusion, avoidance of usual activities, apathy, vomiting, anger, suspicion, high blood pressure, chest pains, problems at work, visual difficulties, isolation, lack of empathy, low productivity, inflexibility, nausea, diarrhea, inability to focus, grinding teeth, insomnia, shallow breathing, sexual problems, spiritual guilt, frantic spiritual searching or seeking magic, poor problem solving, and on. Symptoms range from emotional to physical to spiritual and psychological, and each individual exhibits a unique array of symptoms.

Lay Counselors as Advocates

Advocacy is a political process by an individual or group that aims to influence public policy and resource allocation decisions within political, economic, and social systems and institutions. In the context of our urban community, where crime, poverty, and low education attainment abound, we looked at advocacy in the context of social care: improving access in light of real disadvantages. We looked at it also in the context of inclusion: reconnecting people who have been excluded.

Health advocacy supports and promotes people's health care rights. It enhances these rights through policy initiatives that focus on the availability, safety, and quality of care and community health. It was important to look at what was happening in the broader mental health delivery standards in Philadelphia: positive developments that required us to keep up the momentum. We could see new demand for evidence-based counseling models (pay-for-performance models); a growing demand for professional, faith-based counseling (contextualized services); and a growing demand for specialty in trauma that also understood the role culture played in people's processes when they sought professional services.

What did this mean in our context? Among the mental health leaders in Philadelphia, it meant more collaboration, both civic and professional. The demand for accountability had increased: a demand for tolerance, respect, and fairness. There was recognition that we needed to create

31. Bloom, *Sanctuary*, 19.

opportunities and education, and there was an urgent hunger for justice and respect. Particularly among women, the demand for empowerment had grown, with clients coming in who wanted to deal with their trauma, go back to school, and complete their education. All such initiatives can benefit the wellbeing of people today in providing a high standard of mental health care.

The excessive inequality in our community, however, corroded our growth. It led to a disproportionately high crime rate. The lack of education and the high incidence of crime have only led to sparse employment opportunities and a declining health status in the population. (For more in-depth statistics, refer to chapter 1.)

How did the reality of life in our community impact what we encountered at the Place of Refuge? We conducted an in-house scan of the primary diagnoses across the whole of our clinical activity. Unsurprisingly, the largest diagnosis by far was trauma. The numbers looked a bit like a veteran population—quite telling about the impact of life in our community on the people who were born, lived, and died there. The second- and third-highest diagnoses were depression and anxiety, respectively. (Again, this only represents primary diagnoses.)

The Stages of Treatment

There are three stages in the treatment of trauma, though these stages do not happen in this sequence necessarily; healing involves many twists and turns, but the important thing for the counselor is to recognize these stages as they appear:[32] 1) establishing safety and trust, and forming the therapeutic alliance between the individual and counselor; 2) retelling memories and the process of mourning; and 3) reconnection. In trauma, successful recovery ultimately means reconnecting: a gradual shifting from unpredictable danger to reliable safety.

For stage one, the helper focuses on establishing safety, because the survivor feels unsafe in relationships with others. She both *feels* it and *thinks* it. The survivor also has to feel safe in her body, because her body was attacked. Helping her feel safe in her body often involves teaching how to do self-care for the body, and working together to have a safety plan, re-establishing control over a previously unsafe private world. One of my patients, after many years of counseling, enrolled in a performance school

32. Herman, *Trauma*, 155.

where they taught her how to stand for pictures and helped her groom herself, reestablishing her control over her own body. With many patients, we developed safety plans using an internal form that helped them pick up cues about how they were feeling. When they felt unsafe, we chose things they could do to anchor themselves internally, or we identified a person they felt safe with and could call. The survivor must initiate these interventions, however, because her trauma was forced upon her. In order for her to heal, she must regain control.

A professional counselor will, at this stage, take a full history (biopsychosocial) of the person's family background, social and economic background, spiritual and health care background, and so forth, in order to assess the problem; in lay counseling, some of this probing can be done to help get a full picture of the person.[33]

Stage two requires validating the person's experience. People must talk about what has happened to them, and the talk cannot be sterile; it means talking while living the emotions. The therapist tries to get a "sense," as if watching a movie. Ask: "What do you see, what do you feel, what do you smell?" The counselor must enter into the person's story as a witness. In this stage, the counselor's most important role is to listen—to prompt—to validate the person. Show him he is seen and heard at last.[34]

Once this full process of visiting memory and mourning has passed, we reach stage three: reconnection. Reconnection is when the person can integrate her traumatic history into her total life narrative. She sees what she has been through within the larger experience of humanity. Without denying the horror of her suffering, she can give perspective to this event in the face of the whole. This necessitates finding meaning in what she has suffered—no easy feat.

Any response to trauma eventually boils down to the question, "Why?" One of my patients, arriving at this stage, quoted a passage of Scripture to describe her feelings: "You meant evil against me, but God meant it for good" (Gen 50:20a). She said that, with this foundation, she could move on and become part of the larger community. No suffering is devoid of some meaning and purpose; we do not suffer in vain. But meaning, for the sufferer, often cannot be found in the crucible of pain. Meaning, for the sufferer, comes only after the *shalom* of God abides in the heart.

---

33. Herman, *Trauma*, 165.
34. Herman, *Trauma*, 175.

Module Six: Suicide—Assessment and Treatment

Overview

The training of interns and staff on suicide assessment and treatment was another area we identified as important to our mission. Why? Our immediate community was considered one of the most violent neighborhoods in all of Philadelphia. Loss of life abounded, and the high levels of despair, addiction, and abuse led many people to lose their will to live.

As a professional Christian counselor ministering all of those years in North Philadelphia, I developed a growing knowledge of the affliction that mental illness causes in an individual life. Some years ago, we conducted a study of patients seen at my previous ministry and of the people the center currently served at that time. It was a small but important study, revealing that the two major diagnoses we confronted were depression and anxiety. As a young counselor in the 1990s through early 2010, most of my caseload consisted of individuals who suffered from clinical depression, many of whom struggled with suicide ideation. For several years, most of my active clients were admitted into psychiatric hospitals. In those years, it was hard to be admitted into a local psychiatric ward unless a psychiatrist in an emergency room or a crisis center validated admission. The high hospitalization rate of my active clients informed us that we needed to approach depression and anxiety with clinical excellence and care, but also with every ounce of spiritual discernment and love.

I soon discovered that depression kills. In our community, we ranked among the highest rates of suicides committed in the whole metropolitan area. I saw it daily in our clients of all age groups. Many had such ambivalence about living. Life was too painful; we needed to give them hope. One former client, looking back to her clinical suicidal depression, told me, "I did not want to live when I lost my mother, father, uncles, aunts, cousins, and a few dear friends. Yet through our counseling relationship, God held me when I did not want to hang on." She was a godly woman, truly a follower of Christ; yet with all of the losses in her life, a strenuous job as an emergency telephone operator, financial difficulties, and a divorce caused by repeated abandonment from her spouse, she was forced to push down all of the vulnerability and pain. Many times she misused her prescribed medication for physical pain and depression, and quite often, when appearing for her counseling sessions with me, I could discern that she was high. Over the years, however, as we understood her ambivalence to live and the pain she felt from so many deaths in her family, she slowly regained her emotional strength. Through her relationship with me, we began to seek the Lord. Her life would change for the better when she began to serve others. In fact, she enrolled in a chaplaincy program in a local hospital and was certified as a lay chaplain to minister to seniors in hospitals. For a while this healed her, but only for a period. Her clinical depression returned, though she never again reported suicidal ideation.

We asked her why she thought the depression had lessened in severity, and she referenced two themes: first, that the Hispanic pastor who originally referred her to us gave her his personal cell phone number. This touched her deeply, since she said that her own pastor had never offered such accessibility. Second, she shared that as an African American, her exposure to the very best of our Hispanic cultural strengths—warmth, and a sense of family and inclusion—had reached her heart as nothing else had. Depressed people find that so much of their emotional strength is drained, and they feel incapable of connecting even to those who are closest to their hearts, but this woman found strength in Hispanic ways and culture.

We also noted that prayer was key to her healing, along with providing her a safe and trusting relationship that was embodied by a healthy counseling environment. Much patience and constant care was necessary in this process. I must say, by God's grace, despite our community being at such high risk for suicides, we were protected: in all the time I served there, we did not lose any of our clients. For this reason, the module on suicide became indispensable to our outreach.

Objectives

- To provide lay counselors with an understanding of how suicide assessments are made.
- To provide lay counselors with an understanding of the treatment given to potential suicide victims.

Content

At times, the lay counselor may encounter cases that disturb him. Instinctively, he knows this suffering being shared requires more than just walking alongside the person. He should pay attention to these instincts, because many illnesses *need* professional help. Hearing voices, clinical depression, psychotic behavior, suspicion of child or other abuse—all cases such as these tend to fall outside of what a lay counselor can handle. At that point, he should consult with the lay leader and refer this person to a professional.

This is especially the case with threats of suicide. Our center provided trainees with the following guidelines on suicide assessment given by Douglas Jacobs, associate clinical professor of psychiatry at Harvard.[35]

Suicide Assessment

Multiple contributing factors bring individual people to a suicidal state. The lay counselor should have a basic understanding of the process and methods used by mental health professionals to assess someone who presents with suicidal ideations. Because of suicide's complexity, it requires a thorough examination, identifying both risk factors and protective factors. Attention is given to distinguishing modifiable risk factors from non-modifiable ones. The level of risk (low, moderate, or high) must be determined. A specific suicide inquiry must be made and the assessment documented. Any lay counselor should be aware of these factors in order to make proper referral.

With suicide risk, the counselor must evaluate a number of areas. Any psychiatric illness, such as alcohol/substance abuse, schizophrenia, personality disorder, etc. and any comorbidity of these will be assessed. (In psychology and mental health counseling, *comorbidity* refers to the presence of more than one diagnosis occurring in an individual at the same time. However, in psychiatric classification, comorbidity does not necessarily imply the presence of multiple diseases, but instead can reflect our current inability to supply a single diagnosis that accounts for all symptoms.) The person's medical history, including both personal and/or family history of suicide, is reviewed. The person's coping skills, personality traits, individual strengths, and vulnerabilities will be considered. The person's psychosocial situation—such as acute and chronic stressors, support system (or lack thereof), and religious beliefs—will be assessed. The counselor must give careful consideration to any past and present suicidal ideation, plans, behaviors, intent, anxiety symptoms, and the like.

---

35. Jacobs, "Suicide Assessment."

Risk Factors

Risk factors make up an important part of the person's assessment. These may include monographic information (sex, marital status, age, race, etc.); psychosocial information (employment status, social support, firearm access, etc.); psychiatric diagnosis, comorbidities, and any physical illnesses. The individual's psychological dimensions—hopelessness, psychic pain/ anxiety, turmoil, decreased self-esteem, etc.—are reviewed as risk factors. The therapist also considers behavioral dimensions: impulsivity, aggression, panic attacks, agitation, intoxication, and any prior suicide attempts. The person's cognitive dimensions (such as thought constriction and polarized thinking) are part of risk assessment. Childhood trauma (e.g., sexual and/or physical abuse, neglect, or parental loss) is considered a risk factor as well. And lastly, the family's history of suicide, mental illness, or abuse is included in the assessment.

Protective Factors

Certain protective factors may deter the person from carrying out a threat of suicide. These include such things as the presence of children in the house (except in the case of post-partum psychosis), pregnancy, or religious beliefs regarding suicide. The person may have positive coping skills, life satisfaction, and reality-testing ability. A positive social support system and/or a positive therapeutic relationship are protective factors.

In addition, professional assessment involves an awareness of specific characteristics of a suicide plan. If present, these should be warning signs to the lay counselor and the professional conducting an assessment. Has the person selected the method, the time, and the place to die by suicide? Does the person have available means to do so? It should be noted that firearms at home increase risk as firearms account for 57 percent of suicides.[36]

The psychiatric symptoms most commonly associated with suicide include the following:

1. *Hopelessness*: Research has linked hopelessness and suicidal intent.[37] This is one risk factor that has been shown to be modifiable through various interventions.

---

36. Baker, "Without Guns," 587–88.
37. Beck et al., "Relationship."

2. *Impulsivity/Aggression*: The person's level of impulsivity and/or aggression, regardless of psychiatric diagnosis, forms an important part of assessment, especially in assessing the risk of murder-suicide.

3. *Anxiety*: In a review of inpatient suicides, 79 percent met the criteria for severe or extreme anxiety or agitation.[38] The anxiety symptoms associated with suicide risk include panic attacks, severe psychic anxiety, anxious ruminations, and agitation.

4. *Command hallucinations*: These involve the patient receiving directions from an "inner voice," instructing her to perform certain acts, often dangerous to the self or others. A person having hallucinations of this kind likely has a severe psychotic disorder and would be considered a serious suicide risk. Such a person requires consultation and documentation.

The single most important thing the lay counselor must remember is that *any* suggestion, threat, or mention of a desire to end one's life must be addressed immediately. The counselor must take it very seriously, and action must be immediate. Do not assume that the person "just wants attention." That is not a decision the lay counselor is equipped to make, nor should the counselor undermine the person's expression of ambivalent feelings about life's value. No matter the counselor's personal response, all threats regarding suicide are a serious concern.

Responding to Suicide: Proper Protocol

The correct structure for responding to a potential risk of suicide should include the following:

1. *Immediate referral to the lay leader within the organization.* Lay counselors should know the reporting relationship that has been established within the organization and have the needed contact information.

2. *The lay leader contacts a qualified mental health professional.* This practitioner then conducts a full suicide assessment. He or she should have suicide prevention resources information available. All suicide threats require an assessment and documentation. The goal is to conduct an emergency psychiatric evaluation as soon as possible by a licensed psychiatrist with an MD.

38. Busch et al., "Clinical Correlates."

3. *Establishing the individual's safety.* As the situation unfolds, it is important to keep the person safe. He should not be left alone or placed in circumstances where he has access or means to carry out a suicide. The church or other supporting organization should, if possible, provide needed emergency transportation, contact the family or any significant other who can stay with him, and, if needed, accompany him to the location where the emergency evaluation will be conducted by a licensed psychiatrist or medical provider. If money is needed, the church should be able to make that provision.

4. *Medical assessment is made.* Upon assessment, one of three possible decisions will ensue: admission into a psychiatric facility; release with medication and scheduled outpatient follow-up; or release without medication and scheduled outpatient follow-up.

Module Seven: Cross-Cultural Competency

Overview

The North American mental health schematic solves people's problems through its lens of dominant cultural norms. Until recently, these norms had been developed to help the American middle class, which, until this generation, consisted mostly of white, professional working people. Collectively, these norms also pervade the dominant theories of the leading Christian counseling organizations.[39] Existing secular psychological theories employed to direct Christian counseling methods also serve mostly white, middle-class suburbanites.

Further, mental health professionals incorrectly assume that the lifestyle and experience of the dominant Anglo-Saxon culture are unilaterally adoptable for all Americans. However, value systems and worldviews, which motivate behavior, are not universal. They emanate out of cultural experience; and even in cases of Christian communities, cultural patterns that are biblically based are still uniquely expressed through language, music, custom, emphases, and historical realities.[40] This is true for both

---

39. Today's leading Christian counseling organizations are the Christian Counseling and Educational Foundation and the American Association of Christian Counselors.

40. As Nida says, "The journey into the language of a people leads into the soul of a nation." *God's Word,* 18.

dominant Anglo-Saxon groups within Christianity, as well as marginalized groups like the Hispanic faith communities of my city. Part of the shift needed in both North American mental health and Christian counseling psychologies is to diversify and revolutionize theoretical frameworks and methodologies for the many other cultures found well inside American borders, particularly in the inner city.

As a Hispanic professional, I have spent decades counseling primarily low-income inner-city women and their families, and I have walked with them through the hardships of their daily lives. It has been difficult for me to implement existing counseling psychology while treating psychological symptoms, since my training reflected the norms of middle-class whites. Insight into clients' self-understanding and value system is basic to developing a relevant Christian counseling model.

Since American cities are comprised of multiple interfacing populations, both native-born and immigrant—in the last half of the twentieth century, these have particularly been made of people from Latin American countries[41]—this is an important time for Christian counselors to build new counseling models that will help the newly arrived, socially displaced, unemployed poor from Latin American cities and other countries. Notably, many of these immigrants come from the "two-thirds world," those countries in which the gospel is growing much faster than in the middle-class white culture here in the United States.[42] In some ways, it is more important for urban counselors and educators to immerse themselves in developing a new, relevant vision of culturally sensitive Christian counseling.

Culturally relevant ministries in the inner city can begin to help the new immigrants adjust to American life, and such ministries can continue to assist other groups who have lived in the city for many generations. The poor of our cities need the hope that is found in the gospel of Jesus Christ. As counselors, we knew we could help them find resolutions to their problems and simultaneously witness in meaningful ways as we organized new gospel-centered counseling and community outreaches throughout the city. And as mental health professionals, we invited others to learn with us and apply new theoretical frameworks and counseling methods for the poor in the urban setting. For this reason, we developed the cultural competency module.

---

41. Ortiz, *Hispanic Challenge*, 34.

42. Jenkins, *The Next Christendom*, 89.

Objectives

- To display an understanding of the role worldviews play in behavior and thought.
- To understand some basic components of worldview.
- To grasp the importance, for lay counseling, of identifying one's own worldview.
- To understand how to connect with someone of a different worldview from one's own, especially in counseling.

Content

Cross-cultural competency begins with one's worldview. We recognize our own in order to understand and communicate with others' worldviews. Worldview is "the culturally structured assumptions, values, and commitments or allegiances underlying a people's perception of reality and their responses to those perceptions."[43] Culture can be expressed explicitly and/or implicitly.[44] Explicitly, we can experience the expression of other cultures through their manner of dress, the food they eat, their level of eye contact, or the manner of their greeting. Even the volume at which they speak is a manifestation of cultural norms. Often, expression of initiative is culturally based. Time consciousness too differs widely (between the Hispanics and people of European descent, for example).

Then there are the subjective or invisible expressions of cultural norms. The values of a cultural group take subjective form but can yet be recognized: family ties, work ethic, the importance of education. For example, when Supreme Court Justice Sonia Sotomayor was confirmed, she became the pride and joy not only of her family but of the Hispanic community at large. The collective expression of respect for strong work ethic and education that her confirmation represented was deeply felt by many. Hence, back in her old neighborhood, the tenants supported "The Bronxdale Houses" project in honor of her great accomplishment: "Justice Sonia Sotomayor Houses and Community Center."

---

43. Kraft, *Christianity*, 20.
44. Kraft, *Anthropology*, 134.

Cultural Assumptions

Assumptions play a significant role in cultural development. For example, within many cultures, families assume their children will all get married and have their own children, strongly discouraging the single calling in some instances. The disruption of this cultural assumption can cause division within a family and the community.

Culture drives motivation sometimes in a positive way and sometimes negatively. The community or family that expects its children will do better than their first-generation immigrant parents will see a disproportionate number of college graduates; the urban child who sees the drug dealer driving a sleek car will be motivated to seek the same lifestyle.

Male and Female Behavior

Gender behavior also follows cultural pressure. Hispanic cultures bring with them strong beliefs and assumptions about the roles of men versus women. This is so widely recognized that the term "macho" has become a word used in English conversation and literature to suggest male dominance.

Physical Space

While highly subjective, culture also dictates the physical distance people observe in their interpersonal interactions. We measure and define this distance in three "zones": the social zone, the personal zone, and the intimate zone.

Typically, most North Americans maintain a distance of twelve feet as an acceptable social zone (i.e., the distance one would maintain in a gathering place with strangers). Four feet is the acceptable distance to maintain a personal conversation; one foot is reserved as an intimate zone when interacting with someone with whom one has a close relationship. By contrast, among Hispanic people, these distances shrink: four feet for social interactions; two for the personal zone; and for the intimate zone, touching. In Latin cultures, touching is not only acceptable; it is normal.

Western and Eastern

In this country, whites largely immigrated from European countries and have been classified as "western." Other cultural groups have been classified as "eastern," such as Asians. Hispanic groups share cultural values more closely associated with ethnic groups in the "eastern" classification. An understanding of the contrast between people of European descent and Hispanic cultural values will enhance the lay counselor's perceptions and judgments.

Western or European cultural values place a primacy on independence, on a democratic orientation, and on freedom, as evidenced in the American governmental structure and the "American dream." This culture emphasizes the nuclear family, with less focus on the extended family. It prizes youth over age, and it values traits like assertiveness, competitiveness, and even non-conformity.

By contrast, Hispanic values place strong emphasis on relationships. They stress the respecting of authority. The family is more than the parents and the children; it includes the entire extended family of grandparents, aunts, uncles, cousins, and even those who have been "adopted" into the family (close friends). Interdependence is not only acceptable; it is sought after through the extended family structure. Many members of the extended family may live together, which fosters (in fact, demands) compliance and cooperation. All of this in the Hispanic world provides a sense of security.

Contrasting value systems engender contrasting behaviors. Members of Western cultures grow up seeking to fulfill their own individual needs and taking individual responsibility for their lives. They see themselves as unique and seek self-actualization. Morality is anchored in the individual, and society encourages the expression of feelings. Society also tends to regard time as progressive—ongoing, continuous, advancing step by step.

In the Hispanic world, however, people are taught that they must control their feelings. There is a prescribed way, a uniform way, to behave. Members of society do not reach actualization alone; they reach it through the collective community. Time is treated traditionally, not to be pushed, controlled, or measured. One's life is not a personal adventure but rather a shared experience that must conform to the patterns of the community. Relationships hold a dominant force, acting as the anchor for morality.

Relevance to Lay Counseling

Why does all of this matter for the lay counselor? It matters because the way into a person's soul is through his language—his culture and worldview. Something as practical as connecting with someone in his natural language will connect with his soul, communicating God's word to him where he is. If the lay counselor learns to be attentive to the other person's worldview, she will find points of entry for ministering that she would otherwise have missed.

Finally, for the lay counselor herself, she must acknowledge and decode her own worldview. If she lets her worldview remain unexamined, she risks transmitting judgments onto another's life that are cultural rather than biblical. Attending to this can equip the lay counselor to distinguish between the godly and the universal, and between the cultural and the specific.

Module Eight: Bereavement—Coping with Loss

Overview

Bereavement is a real experience for so many in our communities. Death, homicide, violence, and suicides are some of the tragedies that people live with daily, and this was very much the case in our own community. Therefore, we knew we needed to train any helper in how to approach someone who has lost a loved one, for certainly this was as immediate a problem in North Philadelphia as anywhere else. If we were to be relevant and touch lives, we had to know what hurt and how to respond to the pain in gentleness, with knowledge of the lived reality of the people we were serving.

Objectives

- To increase the lay counselor's awareness of the stages of bereavement.
- To provide strategies for the lay counselor to support the person suffering from loss.

Content

Elisabeth Kübler-Ross, in her 1969 book *On Death and Dying*, first proposed that normal grief involves five stages. She originally applied these stages to people suffering from terminal illness, and she later expanded this theoretical model to apply to any form of catastrophic personal loss (e.g., the death of a loved one, the end of a relationship, divorce, drug addiction, incarceration). According to Kübler-Ross, a person experiencing any of these forms of loss will proceed through these five stages: denial, anger, bargaining, depression, and acceptance.

Denial

Denial works as a defense mechanism that buffers immediate shock. During this period, the individual psychologically blocks the loss. He denies the reality of the situation by ignoring words or hiding from facts. This normal reaction attempts to deal with overwhelming emotions by avoiding them.

Anger

As the masking effects of denial and isolation begin to wear off, reality and its pain re-emerge. Then the person flares up. *I am not ready!* This stage finds the person in the throes of vulnerability. Emotion assaults her vulnerable core, and it is redirected and expressed as anger. At times, though she knows it to be unfair, she may direct her anger at her dying or deceased loved one. Rationally, she knows the person is not to blame; yet still, emotionally, she resents the person for causing her pain or leaving.

Bargaining

Bargaining is a weaker line of defense to protect us from the painful reality. Our normal reaction to feelings of helplessness and vulnerability is to try to regain control. "If only I had sought medical attention sooner . . ." or "If only I had gotten a second opinion from another doctor . . ." or "If only I had tried to be a better person toward my mother . . ." Secretly, we may make a deal with God in an attempt to postpone the inevitable: "If you let my brother live, I promise I'll go to church regularly for the rest of my life!"

Depression

Two types of depression go with mourning; neither, in most cases, can be called clinical depression. Rather, these are natural responses to death—our final enemy—and the counselor should keep in mind that feelings of emptiness and sadness are appropriate during mourning. The first kind of depression is a reaction to the practical implications relating to the loss.

Sadness and regret dominate this type of depression: worry concerning costs and burial, or worry that in our grief we have spent less time with others who depend on us. The second, more subtle and private, is our quiet preparation to bid our loved one farewell. This depression faces the finality of the goodbye: our loved one will never come back. Instead of denying what has happened, depression of this kind faces the reality of our loss.

Acceptance

In this final stage, we learn to cope with the loss. This phase is marked by withdrawal and calm. Rarely is this a period of happiness, but neither is it clinical depression. After the storm has passed, the person continues living with a certain peacefulness and sadness left behind.

The Strategy for Bereavement Support: A Ministry of Silence

In coming alongside someone experiencing natural grief, the counselor's supportive role is a quiet one. The processes of grieving tend to progress naturally. Coping with loss ultimately happens in a deeply personal place, as a singular experience. Nobody can prevent another from going through it or understand all the unique emotions that the grieving person experiences. As a lay counselor, allow the person to grieve fully, not sidestepping or unnaturally curtailing any of these stages. Resisting grief will only prolong the natural process of healing.

In bereavement especially, the counselor must remember to hold himself back, not attempting to fix the pain, nor using clichés (e.g., everything will be okay, it's all right, etc.). One member of our community shared the incredible comfort she experienced, after losing a loved one, when another woman from her church (who had also lost someone) came to her and enveloped her in a quiet hug of understanding. For the bereaved, the ministry of silence holds far more power than words.

In teaching this module, I provided the trainees preliminary descriptions of bereavement and its stages. Then, to supplement with a more pedagogical approach, I brought in a woman from North Philadelphia whose son was murdered. The lay counselors listened to her share her story—her experience of bereavement, her pain—and once she finished speaking, they had the opportunity to talk with her, asking question after question. As lay counselors, what would she have found helpful? What would not be helpful? How did she experience the process of grieving as a Christian?

At the end, we took pictures with her, and everyone prayed for her. Just as with the woman from my church, this woman shared that, during her grieving, she rarely received comfort from others' words. Instead, she found her greatest comfort in a counseling relationship, watching her counselor join her in grieving her child's death. In follow-up discussion, participants shared that the real-life presentation had the profoundest impact on them; grief runs so deeply that there was nothing more powerful than to introduce a real person (with her consent, of course) to see and hear the process first-hand.

There is a place, as well, for reading of the Psalms in times of grief. As I shared in chapter 1, I lost my own brother and sister. Nothing comforted me so much as this ministry of presence, and reading the Psalms. The Psalms appeal not only to the intellect but also to the emotions and will. A project I worked on, translating into Spanish the book *Promesas de Esperanza para Corazones Quebrantados* (*Promises of Hope for Broken Hearts*), utilized the truth of the comfort scriptural lamentation can provide. The book combined passages of Scripture together with work from various local artists, set alongside first-hand accounts from parents who had lost children in our neighborhood. When grieving, there is lamentation in the soul; and great comfort comes from giving that lamentation voice.

A Call to Action

Why Should Christians Enter Lay Counseling?

Certainly the pain in the world around us is evident; we can see the broken and impoverished peoples of the world struggling to survive. *But surely,* we may be tempted to think, *responding to the traumatized is a job for the professionals?* Why should the church seek to lead that task force? Why should ordinary Christians take up the mantle of the lay counselor?

What Does God Say about Our Suffering?

Deny it as they might, the world is looking for the Christian response to suffering—because they want to know how God responds. As Christians, we face a great deal of criticism and condemnation in society, and in many cases, to our shame, we have given good reason for it. We bear the name of God in the world, and when we do not act as God acts—when we do not care for people as God does—we bring shame on God's name.

Somewhere, in the hidden places of people's hearts, they are looking for the light that ought to emanate from the heart of Christians. Slow movement has begun in various circles to look toward religious components to healing, as with the APA, and our city's credentialing agency's tenets that now include faith as a part of holistic health care. These things are a sign that even the federal government is looking to the faith community to lead (or at least become integral partners), and that gives the church an excellent chance to lift Christ high by reaching out to the hurting and offering true, supernatural hope and healing.

Preaching Christ

Often, when the church thinks about evangelism, we imagine preaching on street corners, or handing out tracts, or having theological debates. But there is a way to witness for Christ that looks simpler on the outside, yet reaches far deeper into the hurting human heart—and that is lay counseling. People don't need a "loud faith," as Hudson Taylor put it, a faith that argues or bullies people into joining. They need the touch of God, and they need it most acutely in the worst and most painful parts of their lives.

Those of us who recognize all people as God's children can help deliver that touch. We can look at a man who lost everything—his job, his family, his hope—and show him God's love and light in a time when he feels his whole social position (and therefore his purpose) as his family's provider has vanished. He's no longer looked *to* as the leader, the one who sustains other people. Now he faces weakness, illness, and vulnerability, something that is hard for any human being, but especially for men, who are often trained to believe that their whole worth lies in their provider role, and that they must at all costs never appear weak. In that crucible, feeling lost and directionless, bowed down by shame, we can help his heart once again believe that he can make it. If we reach out to him where he feels helpless, we can strengthen him in faith: faith that he's not going to drown, but that through this time of suffering, God can help him overcome.

We can walk beside the woman—like Maria—who was neglected and abused as a child, living in fear, pain, and poverty. She desperately needs security: to feel safe in her body, first and foremost. Her healing will come out of holy relationships, rooted in the sacredness of the gospel—the good news that God loves this world, loves *us*, so deeply as to become part of it. Modeling that, we can create a space for her of safety and trust. Just as the woman did who came to Jesus in great sadness, poured her costly perfume over his feet, and bathed them with her tears, we can help guide the broken and sorrowing to come to God (Matt 26). In Christ's presence, that woman felt acceptance and respect, and he promised that her story would be told. At his feet, those who have been damaged can at last experience God's healing *shalom*.

Isn't There Too Much Pain?

Why should I bother about doing God's work in this way? the average believer might ask. *Isn't there too much pain for my impact to make any difference?*

The feeling of insufficiency in the face of the world's incredible pain is often the strongest force that keeps God's people from doing divine work. It paralyzes the compassionate heart and discourages the eager laborer. Yet I believe that our task as believers is not to save the world—that is the Savior's job. We're not saving lives in the way God does. But as we follow the living Savior, we serve as Christ's body. We are his hands and feet to the hurting. Our job is simply to obey: to go, to reach out. God will care for the weight of the world.

I understood this in a deeply spiritual way the other day. A young girl knocked on my door. I didn't want to open it; evening was approaching, a big snowstorm was coming, and outside it was horribly cold. Since I live alone, I also tend to take extra care about safety and do not often open the door to strangers. But somehow, that night, I was moved by the Spirit of God, looking out and feeling badly that this girl was out in the cold. So I opened my window and spoke to her where she stood on my porch.

I invited her inside, but she regretfully said that, as she represented a telephone company, policy forbade her from entering my house. She would have to stand by the door as we spoke. I went and got her a footstool to sit on, and since I had been thinking about switching, we exchanged information.

While we spoke, my heart was moved to compassion for her. "May I offer you some hot tea or coffee?" I asked. "It is a cold night for you to be out. I have some cookies as well, if you would like."

She looked up at me in gratitude. "Oh, yes, please, I would really appreciate that!"

From that point on, God moved in on the visit. I could sense God's presence as we talked together. At one point, she said she didn't know what it was, but she felt such peace at my house. People who came to Refuge often said the same. She felt reluctant to leave and told me she had to work until 8 p.m. that night in the cold. "You have been the best customer I've had," she said simply. As she turned to go, I asked her to wait. "You've been so helpful to me," I said. "I'd like to help you in return. I'm a Christian, and I wonder if I can pray for you about anything?"

She smiled in surprise. "Maybe for a few more customers," she said. Then she paused, and added, "And for perseverance in the cold." We prayed together briefly, and I sensed that this girl had an encounter with kindness and loving human interaction that night, such that neither she nor I will forget that experience.

That night, I remembered a great and profound truth. We do not have to be great theologians or experts in neuroscience and psychology to do good in the world. Neither do we need to solve all the world's problems. That beautiful interaction, simple and straightforward, reminded me of what true Christianity is: cookies and coffee, a warm place, human kindness that gave just a little encouragement in the midst of the frozen darkness of loneliness. When Jesus returned from death, one of the first things he did was prepare breakfast on the beach for his disciples (John 21). This, then, is the simplicity of the gospel: *Are you hungry, or cold? Do you need to express the anguish of your soul to someone, to have someone listen to you? Perhaps in that moment, my hand can be the one to offer the bit of bread, the cool drink, the warm embrace, or the listening ear.*

Our involvement will surely fall short of perfect. We will not always know how to show empathy. Especially for those who have been traumatized, our kind gestures could be misconstrued, leading to fear and hypervigilance. We could trigger someone's pain by accident. This presents a great challenge to those who want to minister. But even facing setbacks such as these is often far better than not reaching out at all. When we fall, or when we unintentionally hurt where we meant to comfort, we can learn to speak about it, mend, and grow from the experience.

What If We Do Not Help?

If we refuse to follow our Savior into the dark places, we will see a collapse. Trauma is not an individual affliction; it affects the whole family and community. Fathers and mothers ill and unable to work; people in painful marriages; individuals with a past of abuse: if people such as these do not get the help they need, they may falter and fall. The implications on the way they parent, on the way they form relationships, and on the way they exist as neighbors, employees, helpers, and friends has a ripple effect in society and sets the course for the next generation. Once we grasp that one person's pain affects us all, we will feel the importance of lay counseling. As far as we can make a difference, the lay counselor holds it together for people who cannot do so on their own. In this way, the church helps by reversing the negative effects of suffering that can be devastating to an individual, the trauma that leaves deep imprints of suffering in a person's life.

Suffering people look desperately for help, grasping for strength outside of themselves. Sometimes, by the time clients came to us at Refuge, they had tried everything they possibly could, any path they believed offered healing. They courted addiction to drugs or alcohol; they buried themselves in relationships and sexual fulfillment—good, as God created it, but unable to fully satisfy—or they plunged into materialism, believing that if they acquired wealth, status, belongings, or dressed a certain way, their lives would make sense.

God can use any of these dead-end roads to lead them to the truth of the gospel. When it becomes clear that the thing she chased cannot satisfy, it is then that the hurting woman needs to see the light of Christ, set high like a city on a hill. When he realizes that his pain cannot be fully escaped or drowned out by any of the means he has tried, it is then that the man desperately needs to find the fragrance of Christ that promises rest and *shalom*. When a person like this meets a lay counselor, someone who, by God's grace, can embody the gospel, this person has begun to meet true healing. What more important work could there be for those who love Christ and are called by God's name?

The Joy of Service

We simply cannot have Christianity without following Christ into the suffering of humanity. It cannot exist. If we do not use our bodies, exercising, eating, and sleeping, we become lethargic. In the same way, the church can grow lethargic if it neglects the active service of the God who suffers with us. Living comfortably somewhere, far removed from the pain of the world, does not coexist with fulfilling the purpose of God.

We know, then, that we have an imperative to enter the service of God, and to help deliver the message of good news and healing to the hurting.

But in answering that imperative, sometimes Christians miss out on the joy of it. As Samuel Rutherford writes:

> Believe me, brother, I give it to you under mine own hand-writ, that whoso looketh to the white side of Christ's cross, and can take it up handsomely with faith and courage, shall find it such a burden as sails are to a ship or wings to a bird. I find that my Lord hath over-gilded that black tree, and hath perfumed it, and oiled it with joy and gladness.[45]

For the believer who undertakes this work, laboring not in the dark shadow of the cross, but in its light, the work itself becomes a source of joy.

The gospel says that we must die to self, to our natural human tendencies—our ego, pride, lust, and selfishness—so that we can be born of the spirit and of Christ. I don't see any other way but through encountering the suffering of the world, rather than avoiding or ignoring it. Before my years of service in North Philadelphia, I lived for myself. I was young and could have taken my life in any number of different directions. But the Lord called me to be exposed to suffering, and that exposure has transformed me, because I have learned to die a little at a time, saying no to many selfish pursuits.

A life spent in God's service might look like a life without pleasure or reward, but I have found it to be quite the opposite. I feel that I have been given the treasure Isaiah speaks of, the treasure of darkness (Isa 45:3)—the beauty of Jesus himself in my relationship with him, and the taste of eternal things. The joy that comes from knowing God lives, and lives inside of me, cannot be described.

In doing God's work, we see all the interventions that the Lord provides in people's lives on an ongoing basis. We get, as it were, a front row seat to redemptive work. Most often that work happens in little bits and pieces—not huge, thunderous acts, or miraculous interventions. Often, only those who walk the whole road with another can see God's hand at work. There's a persevering, an everyday, obedient, step-by-step component to Christ's work among the marginalized, and the lay counselor who enters into persevering relationship with the wounded gets to see the Lord's grace, provision, and presence in the long haul.

45. Rutherford, *Letters*, 129.

Finding Harmony

One precious client had a horrible childhood: orphaned when she was young, raised by a truly evil stepmother (in her case, the stereotype actually represented the truth!), brutally mistreated during her early years, and ultimately pushed to run away as a teenager. She married a mentally ill man who mistreated her also, and (as was expected in her culture) bore him children. She came to me bitter and angry. Yet slowly, over the years, she began to soften; she'd bring little gifts and gradually begin to open up to the staff. Bit by bit, I watched that bitterness and anger dissipate.

One day, she sat down in my office, by then a neat lady in her sixties. She looked at me for a moment in silence, and then she said, "Elizabeth, finally I have inner harmony."

She forgave. She made peace with all her history, all the pain.

Her life did not miraculously become pain-free. No, in the midst of the pain, she found peace, and it came to her through her relationship with me and through Refuge. In our small way, we were able to be a witness of the Lord in her life.

So many others have similar experiences in their past. Through the years, I have grieved knowing that countless numbers of human beings grow up in homes and families without love, no physical affection, no kiss or hug from mama or papa. They grow up starving for human love. Unless you listen to these people's stories, you would never know. They look so put together. Imagine what happens to such a person, starving for affection, who walks into a place like Refuge with its climate of love! Believe me: they will keep coming.

A lay counseling ministry, if well established and planned, run by Christians filled with the spirit of God and equipped with these tools, will bear great fruit, because no one can live without love. (That is not to say, of course, that people who do not profess our faith are not able to love— sometimes, to our shame, they show more love and understanding than the church does!) The people of God must enter into real life as Christ did, coming down from heaven to the troubled earth. God sends us out to do the same as Christ did.

I can understand the temptation of wanting to create a utopia on earth: trying to escape from its trials and live without conflict in an easeful place. Yet our Lord calls us to something higher than our own comfort. God calls us to see ourselves as sojourners and pilgrims, loving and caring for the world, but knowing that we are only passing through, to fulfill the purposes of God for humanity and all created things.

When instead of fleeing the sight of pain we enter into those places that are not comfortable or easy, that is where the Lord waits for us. There, God does one miracle after another to accomplish God's own purposes. Perhaps twenty-five years ago when I started working here, I knew about God. But in the pain of Christ's redemptive work, I have come to know God far more intimately than before. Like Job, I can say without doubt: I know that my Redeemer liveth (Job 19:25 KJV).

Finding Your Calling

Not everyone is called to the gift of lay counseling. If you are a finance person, work with numbers. If you are an engineer, bless the world with those gifts. If you are a theologian, write books. In our urban context, every human effort counts; the people need it. But for all with a gentle and sympathetic heart—especially with a curiosity toward or an interest in counseling—I encourage you to get involved, because the world needs you, and the church needs you, and people need you, especially during our times. We must all answer the call, that call of

> the man who was born and lived like us . . . who turned all the world's values upside down, telling us that it was the weak, not the strong, who mattered; the simple, not the learned, who understood; the poor, not the rich, who were blessed; a man whose cross, on which he died in agony, became the symbol of the wildest, sweetest hopes ever to be entertained, and the inspiration of the noblest and most joyous lives ever to be lived.[46]

Final Thoughts

Ministering in the paradoxical tension of seeing what God has done for humanity through grace, while suffering with those who live alienated from God, requires special discipline. It requires a kind of double vision, a balancing act where the helper keeps one foot in their own spiritual experience and the other in the empty places of pain and daily hardship felt by those they are helping. The faith, hope, and love that speak of God's redemption through the death of Christ remain the foundation for all such work.

46. Muggeridge, *Jesus*, 72.

Christians are not called to build a utopia on earth, but rather to fulfill the cultural mandate for humanity—fruitfulness, stewardship—by building God's kingdom on earth, one heart at a time. Christians from multicultural backgrounds with diverse gifts, talents, and abilities gather to work together for the common good of the community.

God's kingdom in the urban context is at the heart of the matter. With this in mind, in the previous chapters, we provided the necessary social information for our target demographic, giving the historical background of the Puerto Rican community in the United States.

We explored themes of alienation via broken relationships, both vertical and horizontal, within the Hispanic cultural dynamic. These forms of alienation were re-examined through the lens of redemption as revealed through Scripture, and were contrasted with Christianity's own significant history of marginalization, as recorded in Scripture and elsewhere.

We closely examined the theological foundation of creation, the fall, and redemption within the practical daily life experiences of Hispanics living in Philadelphia's inner-city neighborhoods. We then dealt with the scriptural teachings regarding Christian duty to society, the reality of suffering in the Christian experience, and the interplay of suffering and servanthood in Scripture, considering the implications these themes have on counseling work in broken neighborhoods and the responsibility of the church to align itself with the marginalized people groups of the world.

We reviewed the case study of Maria through the lens of various secular counseling models, through the church, and through the Refuge model, focusing on the goodness that is made possible through a harmonious union between science and Scripture. Finally, we presented the biblical theme of God's *shalom* and the blessing it brings to the church and community, as well as including the story of the Refuge model's development, and guidelines for implementing such training within other organizations.

Throughout this book, from the dire picture of brokenness in North Philadelphia to the famine in the church, all of the things we have examined make clear to us our responsibility to help in the transformational work of God in our communities. The common Christian can do a great deal to facilitate this work, even without extensive professional training in trauma counseling.

For each of us, that responsibility and the work involved will take a unique shape. The call of God on my own life's work through the Place of Refuge and elsewhere occurred in the hidden places of my mind and heart in my pilgrimage with God. As it became increasingly clear that I was to be the first director of this new counseling center, I struggled with the weight of the calling, as many have done before me and will do after me. Knowing the extent of the suffering that existed within my community, how could I hope to bring about any change, hope, and peace in people's lives when the damage was so great? And how could I avoid doing this with my own glory or wisdom too much in mind? But as I wrestled, I came to sense the gentle promptings of God's Holy Spirit reminding me: "You are bringing *me* to the people. I am their Refuge."

To the Christian feeling discouraged in the face of great suffering and feeling that working towards healing is pointless, I would share this comfort: over the years, the Lord has shown me that God does not call only one individual to this work. The joy of finding others who want to live this life with you, laboring for God's kingdom on earth—in other words, discovering each other and representing the body of Christ in this world—is a pure delight and a source of strength in continuing counseling work. As Christ's body comes together in unity, the joy of the Lord truly becomes our strength, even in the midst of overwhelming evil.

As I contemplate that everyone is formed in the likeness of Christ, knowing God made every human being with a mission to fulfill, it seems even more vital that everyone should take time to discover what passion and work really makes life worthwhile. Where I found my calling, and where others find theirs, is where they find the love of Christ beat the most deeply in their hearts. I found it in North Philadelphia. When you come in contact with that, you know what your life is truly about, and what your life means as connected to this calling.

These truths have taken deep root in me. Indeed, they are the motivating power for my life. When I look at the great brokenness in my city, I do not see myself saving and fixing everything with my wisdom. Neither do I see a hopeless cause too overwhelming to contemplate. No—instead, I envision men, women, and children, of different ages and ethnic backgrounds, of all walks of life, resting in the everlasting arms of our great triune God, who is our Refuge:

> I do not ask for these only, but also for those who will believe in me through their word, that all of them may all be one, just as you, Father, are in me and I in you, that they also may be in us, so that the world may believe that you have sent me. (John 17:20–21)

Bibliography

"2017 Building a Grad Nation Report." *GradNation.org*, May 3, 2017. https://gradnation. americaspromise.org/report/2017-building-grad-nation-report.

Adams, Carolyn, et al. *Philadelphia Neighborhoods, Division, and Conflict in a Postindustrial City*. Philadelphia: Temple University Press, 1991.

Baker, Susan P. "Without Guns, Do People Kill People?" *American Journal of Public Health* 75, no. 6 (June 1985) 587–88.

Baker, Susan S. *Understanding Mainland Puerto Rican Poverty*. Philadelphia: Temple University Press, 2002.

Beck, Aaron T., et al. "Relationship Between Hopelessness and Ultimate Suicide: A Replication with Psychiatric Outpatients." *The American Journal of Psychiatry* 147, no. 2 (February 1990) 190–95.

Berkhof, Louis. *Systematic Theology*. 4th ed. Carlisle, PA: Banner of Truth, 1949.

Bloom, Sandra. *Creating Sanctuary: Toward the Evolution of Sane Societies*. New York: Routledge, 1997.

Bonhoeffer, Dietrich. *Letters and Papers from Prison*. New York: Touchstone, 1997.

Broomhall, Marshall. *Hudson Taylor: The Man Who Believed God*. London: China Inland Mission, 1929.

Busch, K. A., et al. "Clinical Correlates of Inpatient Suicide." *Journal of Clinical Psychiatry* 64, no. 1 (January 2003) 14–19.

Carmichael, Amy. *Edges of His Ways*. Essex, Great Britain: Talbot, 1955.

Chambers, Oswald. *My Utmost for His Highest*. Grand Rapids, MI: Oswald Chambers, 1992.

Cheydleur, John R. *Called to Counsel*. Carol Stream, IL: Tyndale House, 1999.

Chun-Chung Chow, Julian, et al. "Racial/Ethnic Disparities in the Use of Mental Health Services in Poverty Areas." *American Journal of Public Health* 93, no. 5 (May 2003) 792–97.

Comas-Diaz, Lillian. "Puerto Ricans and Sexual Abuse." In *Sexual Abuse in Nine American Cultures: Treatment and Prevention*, edited by Lisa Aronson Fontes, 31–66. London: Sage, 1995.

Conde-Frazier, Elizabeth. "A Spirituality for a Multicultural Ministry." *Perspectivas* 7 (Fall 2003) 57–91.

Costas, Orlando E. *Christ Outside the Gate: Mission Beyond Christendom*. Maryknoll, NY: Orbis, 1982.

Denton, Nancy A., and Douglas S. Massey. *American Apartheid: Segregation and the Making of the Underclass*. Cambridge, MA: Harvard University Press, 1993.

Bibliography

Dunning, Benjamin H. *Aliens and Sojourners: Self as Other in Early Christianity*. Philadelphia: University of Pennsylvania Press, 2009.

Episcopal Church. *The Book of Common Prayer: And Administration of the Sacraments and Other Rites and Ceremonies of the Church, Together with the Psalter or Psalms of David, According to the Use of the Episcopal Church*. 1789. Reprint. New York: Church Hymnal Corporation, 1979.

Fontes, Lisa Aronson, ed. *Sexual Abuse in Nine North American Cultures: Treatment and Prevention*. London: Sage, 1995.

Hart, Dolores. *The Ear of the Heart: An Actress' Journey from Hollywood to Holy Vows*. San Francisco: Ignatius, 2013.

Hauser, Rick, dir. *Strong Kids, Safe Kids*. Los Angeles: Paramount Pictures, 1984.

Henry, Matthew. "Ephesians 2." In *Matthew Henry's Commentary on the Whole Bible (Concise)*. https://www.biblestudytools.com/commentaries/matthew-henry-concise/ephesians/2.html.

———. "Ezekiel 37." in *Matthew Henry's Commentary on the Whole Bible (Concise)*. https://www.biblestudytools.com/commentaries/matthew-henry-concise/ezekiel/37.html.

Herman, Judith. *Trauma and Recovery: The Aftermath of Violence—From Domestic Abuse to Political Terror*. New York: Basic, 1992.

Jacobs, Douglas. "Suicide Assessment." Presentation, University of Michigan Depression Center Colloquium Series, Ann Arbor, MI, December 19, 2003.

Jenkins, Philip. *The Next Christendom: The Coming of Global Christianity*. New York: Oxford University Press, 2002.

Josephus, Flavius. *The Works of Flavius Josephus (JOE)*. Translated by William Whiston. Auburn and Buffalo, NY: John E. Beardsley, 1895.

Kennedy, Eugene, and Sarah C. Charles. *On Becoming a Counselor: A Basic Guide for Non-Professional Counselors and Other Helpers*. New York: Crossroads, 2001.

Kraft, Charles H. *Anthropology for Christian Witness*. Maryknoll, NY: Orbis, 1996.

———. *Christianity with Power: Your Worldview and Your Experience of the Supernatural*. Ann Arbor, MI: Servant, 1989.

Kübler-Ross, Elizabeth. *On Death and Dying: What the Dying Have to Teach Doctors, Nurses, Clergy, and Their Own Family*. London: Routledge, 1969.

Ladd, George Eldon. *A Theology of the New Testament*. Grand Rapids, MI: Eerdmans, 1974.

Langberg, Diane Mandt. *Counseling Survivors of Sexual Abuse*. Wheaton, IL: Tyndale House, 1997.

Leonard, John. "Celebrating Grace: Ephesians 2:1–10." Sermon, Cresheim Valley Church, Philadelphia, 2013.

Moore, R. Lawrence. *Religious Outsiders and the Making of Americans*. New York: Oxford University Press, 1987.

Muggeridge, Malcolm. *Jesus Rediscovered*. Garden City, NY: Doubleday, 1969.

Murray, John. *Collected Writings of John Murray 2: Systematic Theology*. Edinburgh, Scotland: Banner of Truth, 1977.

Nida, Eugene A. *God's Word in Man's Language*. New York: Harper & Row, 1952.

Ortiz, Manuel. *Hispanic Challenge: Opportunities Confronting the Church*. Downers Grove, IL: Intervarsity, 1993.

Perkins, John M. *Restoring At-Risk Communities: Doing It Together and Doing It Right*. Grand Rapids, MI: Baker, 1995.

Bibliography

Perry, Bruce, and Maia Szalavitz. *The Boy Who Was Raised as a Dog: And Other Stories from a Child Psychiatrist's Notebook*. New York: Basic, 2007.

"Philadelphia 2020 State of the City." *PewTrusts.org*, April 7, 2020. https://www.pewtrusts. org/en/research-and-analysis/reports/2020/04/philadelphia-2020-state-of-the-city.

"Philadelphia's Labor Force." *PhilaWorks.org*, May 25, 2016, https://www.philaworks.org/ philadelphias-labor-force/.

Poythress, Vern. *The Shadow of Christ in the Law of Moses*. Brentwood, TN: Wolgemuth & Hyatt, 1991.

Richard, Earl J. "Honorable Conduct Among the Gentiles: A Study of the Social Thought of 1 Peter." *Word & World* 24, no. 4 (Fall 2004) 412–20.

Richards, P. Scott and Allen E. Bergin. *A Spiritual Strategy for Counseling and Psychotherapy*. 2nd ed. Washington, DC: American Psychological Association, 2005.

Roberts, R. C. "Philosophy of Forgiveness." Presentation, American Association of Christian Counselors, Geneva Institute, Geneva, Switzerland, February 27, 2005.

Rutherford, Samuel. *The Letters of Samuel Rutherford*. Chicago: Moody, 1951.

Selby, Peter. *Grace and Mortgage: The Language of Faith and the Debt of the World*. London: Darton, Longman & Todd, 2009.

Shepherd, Norman. "Law and Gospel in Covenantal Perspective." *Reformation and Revival Journal* 14, no. 1 (2005) 73–88.

Snodgrass, William F. "He Offered Up Himself." In *Resurrection and Eschatology: Theology in Service of the Church: Essays in Honor of Richard B. Gaffin Jr.*, edited by Lane G. Tipton and Jeffrey C. Waddington. Phillipsburg, NJ: P & R, 2008.

Van Til, Cornelius. *The Dilemma of Education*. Phillipsburg, NJ: P & R, 1956.

Volf, Miroslav. *After Our Likeness: The Church as the Image of the Trinity*. Grand Rapids, MI: Eerdmans, 1998.

———. *Exclusion and Embrace: A Theological Exploration of Identity, Otherness, and Reconciliation*. Nashville, TN: Abingdon, 1996.

Watkins, Eric B. "Filling Up Christ's Afflictions: A Sermon on Colossians 1:24–29." In *Resurrection and Eschatology*, edited by Lane G. Tipton and Jeffrey C. Waddington. Phillipsburg, NJ: P&R, 2009.

Weeks, Noel. *The Sufficiency of Scripture*. Carlisle, PA: Banner of Truth, 1988.

Wolterstorff, Nicholas. *Until Justice & Peace Embrace*. Grand Rapids, MI: Eerdmans, 1983.

www.ingramcontent.com/pod-product-compliance
Lightning Source LLC
Chambersburg PA
CBHW061736270326
41928CB00011B/2260